HOT BUTTONS
on
MORALITY

HOT BUTTONS
on
MORALITY
Recovering Foundational Biblical Standards

by
Frank R. Shivers

LIGHTNING SOURCE
1246 Heil Quaker Blvd.
La Vergne, TN

Unless otherwise noted, Scripture quotations are from
The Holy Bible *King James Version*

Library of Congress Cataloging-in-Publication Data

Shivers, Frank R., 1949-
Hot Buttons on Morality / Frank Shivers
ISBN 978-1-878127-15-0

Library of Congress Control Number:
2012900129

Cover design by
Tim King of Click Graphics, Inc.

For Information:
Frank Shivers Evangelistic Association
P. O. Box 9991
Columbia, South Carolina 29290
www.frankshivers.com

To

Dr. Timothy Faulk
An Aaron and Hur to me

"Moses' hands were heavy;...and Aaron and Hur stayed up his hands, the one on the one side, and the other on the other side."
—Exodus 17:12

Content

Preface

"Remove not the ancient landmark, which thy fathers have set" (Proverbs 22:28). This directive was given to the Israelites centuries ago regarding property boundaries between neighbors. Its application today is to be taken spiritually regarding moral and ethical boundaries God has established for man's protection and highest good. These ancient landmarks, though as old as creation, are just as relevant as the day God made their pronouncement.

The removal of or tampering with a property landmark skews what belongs to whom, whereas removal of or tampering with God's spiritual landmarks results in havoc and heartache. The words of Solomon are pertinent and plain. "There is a way which seemeth right unto a man, but the end thereof are the ways of death" (Proverbs 14:12).

Removal or adjustment of a property landmark can be done legally with permission of its owner. The same is true with spiritual landmarks. However, without the consent of God, liberal clergy, psychologists, scholars, teachers, and politicians have been and are constantly moving the marker stakes further from the right. The ancient boundary markers now are blurred due to man's continual tampering.

Hot Buttons on Morality, the second volume in the Hot Buttons series for students, is intended to remove the fog, helping students see the clearly defined boundary markers God has erected regarding issues such as abortion, homosexuality, premarital sex, gambling, alcohol, drugs, suicide, tobacco, parental submission, music, dating, marriage, and divorce. Knowledge of and obedience to the spiritual boundaries divinely established in Holy Scripture will prevent the dishonoring of God and the defilement and devastation of life.

Battle relentlessly any political, cultural, religious, and social efforts to remove God's established moral boundaries (Ephesians 5:11). The great London pastor C. H. Spurgeon said, "We are not to expect to win victories for the Lord Jesus by a single blow. Evil principles and practices die hard. In some places, it takes years of labor to drive out even one of the many vices which defile the inhabitants. We must carry on the war with all our might, even when favored with little manifest success. Our business in this world is to conquer it for Jesus. We are not to make compromises, but to exterminate evils. We are not to seek popularity, but to wage unceasing war with iniquity. Infidelity, drink, impurity, oppression, worldliness, error—these are all to be 'put out.' The Lord our God can alone accomplish this. He works by His faithful servants. Let us never sheathe the sword till the whole land is won for Jesus. Courage, my heart! Go on little by little, for many 'little's' will make a great whole."[1]

To assure comprehension and application, each Hot Button is concluded with an Ask Yourself section for personal and group discussion.

Something cannot be politically right if it is morally wrong.
—Abraham Lincoln

The modern world, because it is indifferent to dogmatic truth, has logically become indifferent to ethical truth.[2]—Bertrand L. Conway

What happens to all of us, unless our powers of moral judgment are acute and alert, is that our understanding of what is "normal" begins to be modified. Under the impression that "everybody does it" and that nobody nowadays believes much in God or in absolutes of truth and goodness, our defenses are lowered, and our values imperceptibly altered. We begin to assume that physical violence (when we are provoked), sexual promiscuity (when we are aroused), and extravagant consumer expenditure (when we are tempted) are the accepted norms of western society. We have been conned.[3]—John Stott

At the foundation of a person's life, we find his beliefs. These beliefs shape his values, and his values drive his actions.[4]
—Glen Schultz

If you find yourself loving any pleasure better than your prayers, any book better than the Bible, any house better than the house of God, any table better than the Lord's Table, any person better than Christ, or any indulgence better than the hope of Heaven—take alarm.[5]—Thomas Guthrie

"And thine ears shall hear a word behind thee, saying, This is the way, walk ye in it, when ye turn to the right hand, and when ye turn to the left."—Isaiah 30:21.

Chapter 1   Pornography

"I will set no wicked thing before mine eyes."—Psalm 101:3.

I am emotionally involved. My addiction to pornography paralyzes my spiritual life, perverts my view of the world, distorts my social life, destroys any possibility of God using me; and I just can't stop. Lust eats me up, yet it doesn't satisfy. Pornography promises me everything; it produces nothing.—A Porn Addict

Perhaps the most obvious injury from pornography occurs in the mind. Once porn is downloaded into our mental hard drive through the portals of the senses, it works like a computer virus, corrupting our thoughts about sexuality. The contaminated files include our thoughts about being male or female, what we believe about our sexuality, how we plan to behave sexually, and whether we have the capacity to remain faithful in marriage.[6]—Rob Jackson

Sixty-seven percent of eighteen- to twenty-six-year-old men believe viewing pornography is acceptable, whereas in that same age bracket, forty-nine percent of women do.[7] Ninety percent of students aged eight to sixteen have viewed pornography on the Internet.[8]

Every second, $3,075.64 is being spent on pornography.
Every second, 28,258 Internet users view pornography.
Every second, 372 Internet users are typing adult search terms into search engines.
Every 39 minutes, a new pornographic video is being created in the United States.[9]

Pornography is escalating, and in its path it leaves degradation, perversion, addiction, and destruction of young lives.

1

Precept against Pornography

"Flee fornication" (1 Corinthians 6:18). The Greek word rendered "fornication" is *porneuo* (porn-*yoo*-oh) which means "to engage in illicit sexual intercourse, play the harlot, and prostitute oneself." *Porneuo* is a generic word in Greek that covers all forms of sexual impurity. If one compares the word *pornography* with *porneuo,* it is easy to see the connection; the first fuels the action of the other. Both are condemned in Scripture. Pornography at its root violates a scriptural principle governing conduct. Paul the Apostle states in 1 Corinthians 10:31, "Whether therefore ye eat, or drink, or whatsoever ye do, do all to the glory of God." One certainly cannot view pornographic material "to the glory of God."

Power of Pornography

Don't underestimate the power of pornography. Just as an ocean begins with a drop of water, even so a captive life to pornography begins with a first glance. What harm is there in pornography?

It *derails* your walk with God. You cannot serve two masters (Matthew 6:24). In serving pornography, intimacy with God decays, and your walk becomes cold and distant.

It *distorts* God's view of sex. Sex is intended to be shared between a husband and wife. Pornography distorts the mind into believing that any form of sex is acceptable at any time.

It *devours* peace. Pornography leads to shame and deep guilt that robs one's inner peace and joy.

It *destroys* life. Pornography fuels the heart with such lustful passion that it can lead to acts of violence to satisfy its craving. According to an FBI study, eighty-one percent of sex murderers said their biggest sexual interest was pornography.[10] Pornography may lead to the sexual exploration and devastation of children. Dr. Elizabeth Holland warns about the relationship between pornography and child molestation: "There exist in our nation...those men and women who have been abused, who have been damaged for life by those who feed on pornography...who have a sickness, who need to feed on dirty pictures and pornography; and when touching pictures and fantasizing and looking no longer satisfy these people's insatiable appetites, they move on. And they move to live children. I know, because I treat these children."[11]

It *depreciates* women. Pornography is primarily a man's business. It degrades women into sex objects.

It *dominates* the mind. Pornography masters the will, taking one prisoner. The visual stimulus of pornography causes a chemical to be secreted which locks the pleasing image into the mind and reinforces the body's own desire to repeat the process.[12] "These memories," states Victor Cline, "very vivid and graphic in nature, keep intruding themselves back on the mind's memory screen, serving to stimulate and arouse the viewer."[13]

Dr. James L. McDough states, "Experiences at times of emotional or sexual arousal get locked in the brain by the chemical epinephrine and become virtually impossible to erase."[14] The "inerasable" imprints pornography forges upon the mind make deliverance from its clutches extremely difficult at best. "One in ten Internet pornography users will become compulsive," states Dr. Al Cooper of Stanford University. He explains, "The physiological reaction to Internet pornography is similar to what a cocaine user would experience."[15]

It *dupes* you. It deceives you into believing that what once was thought abominable, gross, and repulsive is really acceptable. Numbness to the most graphic pornography may develop.

It *disrupts* marriage. Pornography leads to an unhealthy expectation regarding sex in marriage. Its pictures, movies, and magazines mar normal and healthy marital sexual expectations.

It *damages* one's reputation. Pornography injuries the believer's witness and testimony.

It *depletes* a person's time and energy. Endless hours and energy can be exhausted searching for that "right" picture on the Internet or in magazines. It robs one of time and energy that should be spent in studying for class, in Bible study, or in wholesome activities with family and friends.

Pornography will take you further than you want to go. It will keep you longer than you want to stay. It will cost you more than you want to pay. Freedom from the clutches of pornography takes serious action, beginning with a repentant heart unto God.

Freedom from Pornography

A nineteen-year-old male testified, "Pornography is like a parasite, draining the goodness and life out of me, slowly but surely turning me into some instrument of decadence that I myself cannot recognize. I only pray that God has mercy on my soul and gives me the strength to break free." How can one shackled to the prison chains of pornography be set free?

It takes *desire*. A casual attitude about disengaging pornography in your life will not bring about its defeat. Freedom begins with a heart that sincerely says, "Enough is enough." The comical definition of insanity is "doing the same thing again and again, yet expecting a different result." You can't keep doing what you are doing and expect things to be any different.

It takes *decision*. In addition to a firm decision to quit pornography, one must decide *for* Christ. The darkness of pornography must and will give way to the Light of Jesus Christ *in you*. This decision either involves the yielding of your life to Him as Lord and Savior or, if you are already a believer, anew to Him in Lordship.

It takes *devotion*. Feed your mind on the Word of God; burn its truths into your heart (Psalm 119:11). Engage in persistent and passionate prayer, for that links you to Divine power needed to thwart this temptation. Pray specifically that Jesus will keep you from "the evil one" (Matthew 6:13 ASV).

It takes *dependence*. Rely upon Christ for power to withdraw and resist (John 8:36). You have natural strength; Satan has supernatural strength; but Jesus has super-duper-natural strength (Philippians 4:13)! Rely upon fellow believers as you fight pornography, asking them to hold you accountable (Galatians 6:1–2).

It takes *discipline*. In order for the nation of Israel to be set free from idol worship, they had to "cut down" the groves of Baal (Judges 6:25). As long as these groves remained, Israel would have opportunities to slip back into idolatry. "Cut down" the opportunities to engage in pornography, or else they will serve only as a temptation to stumble. Delete pornography files from your computer; discard pornographic magazines stashed in a secret place; burn porn-rock videos. Set out to win, not lose (Ephesians 4:27; 2 Corinthians 10:4–5).

It takes *determination*. In Southern Europe, the white ermine is hunted for its beautiful white fur. The hunter locates the ermine's home and pours tar at its entrance. He then releases the dogs that pursue the ermine. The ermine flees to its home but finds the tar and refuses to trample through the tar to safety. It would rather die than defile its beautiful white fur. Exhibit the resolve of the ermine in fighting pornography. Determine never again to be polluted with the filthy, black tar of pornography.

Ask Yourself

Do you see anything wrong with the viewing of pornography? Why or why not?

Are you viewing pornography in any form by any media?

Do you hide pornographic searches on the Internet from family and friends? Why?

What consequences has such viewing had upon your life?

How does being a Christian mesh with a pornographic appetite?

Are you held captive in the clutches of pornography, and, if so, isn't it time to be set free? Freedom from its grip will only become more difficult the longer you delay.

Do you know of another who is struggling with pornography? How might you help this person see its devastating consequences and be set free?

List five consequences of viewing pornography.

Jer- 1: 4- 10

Chapter 2   Abortion

"For you formed my inward parts; you knitted me together in my mother's womb. I praise you, for I am fearfully and wonderfully made. Wonderful are your works; my soul knows it very well. My frame was not hidden from you, when I was being made in secret, intricately woven in the depths of the earth. Your eyes saw my unformed substance...."—Psalm 139:13–16, ESV.

One of the darkest days in American history [the date of the Roe v. Wade opinion, January 22, 1973], a day, in my estimation, like Pearl Harbor, a day that will live in infamy.[16]—Adrian Rogers

Since when does anyone's right to live depend upon someone else's wanting them? Killing the unwanted is a monstrous evil....So, should a woman have the right to choose? I have a right to free speech, but not to shout "fire" in a theater. A person's right to anything stops when it injures or kills another living human....The pivotal question is, should any civilized nation give to one citizen the absolute right to kill another to solve the first person's personal problem?[17]—John Willke

even Before iN the eyes of God

Life begins at the moment of conception in the womb; baby Tom or Jen is not a mass of tissue, but a living being created by God. Outside the Bible, this truth is also documented in embryology textbooks in which you may read about the developmental life of the embryo and fetus. Ultrasound images of a child in the womb also render confirmation that life begins at conception. As much as I detest the word abortion, it accurately describes what happens the moment the doctor terminates the unborn child; the procedure (horrific as it is) aborts the wonderful life of a Tom or Jen that God created. The aborted one will never have the chance to go to school

7

or to the junior-senior prom, will never get married and live the American dream. As for them and the millions of others who die in the womb at the "choice" of their mothers and/or fathers due to no wrong of their own, it is "Mission Aborted"; God's purpose for their lives has been savagely vetoed.

In 2003, nearly one in three pregnancies in America ended in an abortion.[18] Eighty-six percent of these ladies who opted for an abortion cited their reasons as "not ready for a child," "can't afford a baby," or "would interfere with education or career plans."[19] In essence, these chose to end the lives of their children out of selfishness—having the child would be too big an inconvenience.

Laura Ingraham states, "The 'right to choose' has for thirty years been a smokescreen for aborting unwanted children, but these days it is taking on a more literal meaning, along with the expression 'family planning.' It turns out the 'right to choose' and family planning aren't just about *how many* children you have anymore. It's about how tall your children are, what sex, and certainly whether or not they have any disabilities. For now, the tools of this new family planning are the same, though—you abort the ones who don't match your wishes."[20]

In excess of ninety-five percent of the abortions performed today [2011] involve women who simply do not want to have a child.[21] The killing of a precious child because he or she would interfere with someone's personal agenda or due to his or her health or appearance is abhorrent in a civilized society.

The Bible consistently uses the same Greek word *(brephos)* to describe an unborn child, a newborn child, and a young child. In Luke 1:44, it is used to describe the unborn child; in Luke 2:12, it refers to the newborn child; and in Luke 18:5, it means a young child.[22] Why? It is because the God of the Universe sees no biological difference in a child inside the womb or outside the womb; they are both human beings. The Bible emphasizes the fact that the unborn child is known and valued by God. "Before I formed you in the womb I knew you, and before you were born I consecrated you" (Jeremiah 1:5, ESV). "I am fearfully and wonderfully made....My frame was not hidden from you, when I was being made in secret, intricately woven in the depths of the earth Your eyes saw my unformed substance..." (Psalm 139:14–16, ESV).

Why doesn't the Bible specifically condemn abortion (i.e. "Thou shalt not abort a child.")? One major reason is that its prohibition is enveloped in the sixth commandment: 'Thou shalt not murder.' Israelites clearly understood this command to include killing by sword, poison, strangulation, abortion, and all other means.[23] The same punishment was to be inflicted upon one for killing an unborn child or an adult (Exodus 21:22–25), showing again that God sees the unborn person as a human being. The early church embraced the same view. "Thou shalt not slay the child by procuring abortion; nor, again, shalt thou destroy it after it is born."[24] It is man's selfishness and degradation that has spawned cultural acceptance of abortion. This holocaust of the unborn must stop. Protect the unborn. Speak up for adoption and against abortion.

> It's in His image they're created,
> Each one a precious gift of life;
> How can we steal away their future?
> What gives us the power? What gives us the right?[25]

There is no legitimate "pro-choice" position, according to Scripture. The alternative to abortion (outside of bearing and rearing the child) is adoption. One and one-half million Americans desire to adopt a child, so there is no such thing as an "unwanted child."

All sins are forgivable by a loving God, including that of abortion (1 John 1:7–9; Isaiah 43:25–26). The Christian's response to women who have an abortion, men who encourage abortion, and the medical team who perform the abortion is disdain for what they did, yet with open arms to forgive, heal, and restore in Jesus' name (Galatians 6:1; Luke 17:3).

ASK YOURSELF

At what point does life begin in the womb?

Why doesn't the Bible specifically condemn abortion?

How does the use of the same Greek word for the unborn, newborn child, and young child in Scripture reveal God's view that life begins at conception?

Long before abortion became a legal issue, it was (and remains) a moral one. Explain.

Does society's sanctioning of abortion make it right?

What can you do to speak up for the unborn child?

What is the alternative to abortion?

How might you counsel a friend who just had an abortion and is grieving because she did?

Where do a woman's rights end and a baby's rights begin?

View "180" (180movie.com).

Chapter 3   Homosexuality

"If the Son therefore shall make you free, ye shall be free indeed."—John 8:36.

Homosexuality is the manifestation of sexual desire toward a member of one's own sex or the erotic activity with a member of the same sex. (The Greek word *homos* means "the same"). A lesbian is a female homosexual.[26]—Lehman Strauss

From start to finish, Scripture categorically condemns same-sex intimacy.[27]—Max Lucado

A male teen struggling with homosexual desires made a statement to this effect: "I just wish the preacher would talk about it." His statement expressed desire not only to know the biblical view of homosexuality but the way of escape from its bondage. You may identify with him or know someone who does.

Is homosexuality wrong? The standard of conduct morally and ethically is not culture, public opinion or the laws enacted by man, but the Bible. The Bible is the final authority on right and wrong, and it vetoes every act of congress or church that violates God's divine design for man and woman sexually. Therefore, in order to answer the question posed, one needs to check out what God states about homosexuality in the Bible.

In Leviticus 18:22 (NLT), God declared, "Do not practice homosexuality, having sex with another man as with a woman. It is a detestable sin." In Leviticus 20:13 (NLT), God stated, "If a man practices homosexuality, having sex with another man as with a woman, both men have committed a detestable act." Again, God said, "There shall be no whore of the daughters of Israel, nor a sodomite of the sons of Israel" (Deuteronomy 23:17). The word "sodomite" in this text does not refer to the inhabitants of Sodom, but to men who engage in the same deviant, perverted homosexual conduct that the men in Sodom practiced. Check out further teaching about this sin in the New Testament (Romans 1:24–27; 1 Timothy 1:10; 1 Corinthians 6:9–11 and Jude 7). Though Jesus didn't speak out against homosexuality directly, it is crystal clear that He opposed it, as He opposed rape, incest, bestiality, and child abuse, although He never referred directly to any of them either. Jesus validated, supported the Old Testament laws on sexual behavior, which clearly prohibited homosexuality (Matthew 5:27–30). Jesus also spoke of sexuality in the context of a lifelong heterosexual commitment between a male and female (Matthew 19:4–9). Homosexuality is clearly condemned by Jesus as an act that is abominable and perverted. A person is not *homophobic* for embracing a biblical stance against homosexuality.

People are not born homosexual (not a biological gene thing) but become homosexual due to abuse or some other factors during their development. The bottom line is that neither you nor others have to be gay. There is a way out. Perhaps you have struggled with homosexual feelings since childhood, unable to change despite repetitive serious attempts. Today, right now, all that can change.

Being Set Free

How can you or someone you know be freed from the homosexual lifestyle? Recognize that homosexuality is a deviant act condemned by God and acknowledge it as sin. Next, enter into a personal relationship with Jesus Christ by confessing the sin (and all sin), turning from it and inviting Him into your life as Lord and Savior (Acts 20:21; Romans 10:9–13). It is impossible to defeat the sin of homosexuality or any other sin apart from Christ's enablement (Jeremiah 32:27).

For believers captive to this vice, deliverance encompasses three things: renunciation (*renounce*: to formally declare one's abandonment of; refusal to recognize or abide by it any longer[28]), repentance (*repentance:* an about face, change of direction of conduct involving confession of sin to God with godly sorrow), and renewal (*renewal:* mental and spiritual heartfelt submission to the control and authority of Jesus Christ, involving restored spiritual strength and the pursuit of holiness) (Romans 12:1–2).

Upon acknowledging, confessing, and being cleansed by God for homosexual behavior, don't look or turn back. With Paul the Apostle, I say, "Stand fast therefore in the liberty wherewith Christ hath made us free, and be not entangled again with the yoke of bondage" (Galatians 5:1).

Stand fast in this new freedom by **devotion.** Mediate upon and memorize the Word of God. David declared, "Thy word have I hid in mine heart, that I might not sin against thee" (Psalm 119:11). Don't simply *read* it, but *heed* it (Psalm 119:9) that you may remain clean. Scripture verses will keep you from spiritual reverses. Intimacy with God is essential to maintaining freedom.

Stand fast in this new freedom by **disconnection** and **deprivation**. Delete stored pornographic websites, videos and/or pictures. Cut yourself loose from people who tempt you to return to the old life. Give no "place to the devil" (Ephesians 4:27). Deprive the flesh of all eye candy.

Stand fast in this new freedom by **determination**. Don't stop the fight with this sin until it is totally driven out of the heart! If you fall down, don't use that as an excuse to stay down, but immediately get back up!

Stand fast in this new freedom by **dependence** upon God and man. Seek out a godly pastor, student minister, or friend to hold you accountable to a conduct of purity on a weekly basis. Develop healthy friendships with heterosexual men who under-stand the struggle. Seek counsel from a minister or therapist who can assist in total deliverance based upon Christian principles.

Stand fast in this new freedom by pondering the **danger.** When you are tempted to return to the homosexual lifestyle, ask yourself if the temporary gratification of the flesh is worth the heartache, havoc, and hellishness that it produces.

Stand fast in this new freedom by **discipline.** Forget yesterday and its sins. Paul declared, "But I focus on this one thing: Forgetting the past and looking forward to what lies ahead, I press on to reach the end of the race and receive the heavenly prize for which God, through Christ Jesus, is calling us" (Philippians 3:13–14 NLT). Bury yesterday and leave it buried.

Deliverance will be a struggle, as it is for one with a drug or alcohol addiction, but it is attainable. Take it one day at a time. Concentrate on winning the battle TODAY. Never doubt God's love or ability to set you free.

Testimonials abound of students once entrapped in the vice grip of homosexuality who now live healthy heterosexual lives. Transformations such as these provide documentation that all who are captive to this sin may be delivered by the grace of God.

"Don't you realize that those who do wrong will not inherit the Kingdom of God? Don't fool yourselves. Those who indulge in sexual sin, or who worship idols, or commit adultery, or are male prostitutes, or practice homosexuality, or are thieves, or greedy people, or drunkards, or are abusive, or cheat people—none of these will inherit the Kingdom of God. *Some of you were once like that* [italics added]. But you were cleansed; you were made holy; you were made right with God by calling on the name of the Lord Jesus Christ and by the Spirit of our God" (1 Corinthians 6:9–11 NLT). You can join the ranks of the *"Some of you were once like that"* crowd by the grace of God today.

The Christian's Role

Christians do great injustice and disservice to homosexuals who are seeking deliverance in simply telling them to "stop doing it." They already want to "stop doing it," or they never would have sought help (as it is with drug, alcohol, and pornography addicts); it's the *means* of freedom that they seek. If you are unable to help them, then point them to qualified spiritual counselors (pastors, student ministers) and/or Christian psychological professionals.

"Some homosexuals," states Max Lucado, "hate Christians because they think Christians hate them. I honestly cannot imagine what it must be like to hear Christians shout, 'Stop your sinning! You are a sinner!' To be called 'fag' or 'queer' by people who claim to follow Jesus—travesty! This treatment is tragic and wrong." Lucado continues, "Were Jesus to come face to face with a homo-sexual, what would He say? What would He do?...He would express love. He would speak to them with compassion. But He would also speak to them with conviction."[29] Lucado said that Jesus would tell them the truth clothed in these three things, and the truth is this. God disapproves of same-sex intimacy.[30] The Christian must respond in the same way.

A Rutgers University student secretly filmed and then posted on the Internet his roommate's homosexual activity. The roommate, eighteen-year-old Tyler Clementi, in turn committed sui-cide by jumping off the George Washington Bridge in Manhattan. Suicide is the leading cause of death among gay and lesbian youth in America; conservatively, the number of gay and lesbian student suicides annually in America is 1,500.[31] One but wonders how many of these students yet would be alive had Christian youth countered the bullying (cyberspace or otherwise) that played a major role in their suicide with compassion (despite opposition to and detesta-tion for the sin), providing hope and support in the name of Jesus Christ. The Christian possesses the Key that unshackles the captive to Satan, setting him free to a new life—that Key is a personal relationship with Jesus Christ.

ASK YOURSELF

What is homosexuality?

Is its practice right or wrong? Why?

Explain the following statement: Couched in God's displeasure with homosexual behavior is His love for the offender.

Do you or does someone you know struggle with homosexuality?

Is there any hope for the homosexual being set free, and, if so, how?

If caught up in this sin, did you pray the prayer cited? If so, what happened?

If you are battling homosexual conduct, have you contemplated suicide?

Why is suicide not the answer to defeating homosexuality?

What is the Christian's response to homosexuality and to the homosexual?

What do the alarming statistics regarding suicide among homosexuals clearly reveal?

For testimonials of former homosexuals and additional support, contact Exodus International (exodusinternational.org).

16

Chapter 4   Same-Sex Marriage

"For this reason a man will leave his father and mother and be united to his wife, and they will become one flesh."—Genesis 2:24, NIV.

In the beginning, God created Adam and Eve, not Adam and Steve.

Marriage is a sacred union, ordained by God to be a life-long, sexually exclusive relationship between one man and one woman. History, nature, social science, anthropology, religion, and theology all coalesce in vigorous support of marriage as it has always been understood: a life-long union of male and female for the purpose of creating stable families.[32]—Focus on the Family

It has been said, "Before you remove a fence, you need to ask why that fence was erected in the first place." Over 6,000 years ago, God erected the fence of marriage between a man and woman for good reason, and now an attempt is underway to remove it. Same-sex marriage is simply a counterfeit of God's heavenly design for marriage that cheapens and degrades the real thing.

Dr. James Dobson, Focus on the Family Founder, stated, "And that's why it [same-sex marriage] will destroy marriage. It will undermine the traditional relationship between men and women. It has happened in the Netherlands. Young people are not getting married. When you go in that direction, you confuse the meaning of marriage, and then it is destroyed. The family is destroyed. That is the foundation for Western civilizations, and I tell you it will bring the destruction of this nation and many others, if we go in that direction."[33]

What does the Bible say about marriage? It was instituted by God (Matthew 19:3–4). It was designed for male and female (Matthew 19:4). In marriage, man and woman become one flesh through the sexual union (Matthew 19:5). In marriage, it is God that joins the couple together, not the church or state (Matthew 19:6). Marriage is a lifetime commitment (Matthew 19:9). The big point the Bible makes about marriage is that it takes place between a man and a woman (1 Corinthians 7:3–4; Romans 7:1–4; Ephesians 5:22–33; Colossians 3:18–19; 1 Timothy 3:2,11–12; 5:14; Titus 1:6; 2:4–5; 1 Peter 3:1–7). Never once is marriage referred to in scripture as consisting of two people of the same sex.

"Adam was alone and in need of a suitable mate," writes John MacArthur. "Therefore God's final act of creation on day six— the crowning step that made everything in the universe perfect— was accomplished by the forming of Eve from Adam's rib. Then 'He brought her to the man' (Genesis 2:22). By that act, God established the family for all time. The Genesis narrative says, 'Therefore a man shall leave his father and his mother and hold fast to his wife, and they shall become one flesh' (v. 24). Jesus quoted that verse in Matthew 19:5 to underscore the sanctity and permanence of marriage as an institution."[34]

John Edmiston states: "When God created a partner for Adam, He created Eve—not another Adam. This means that perfect partnership requires some level of difference as well as a level of similarity, so great that Adam could cry out loudly, 'This is now bone of my bones and flesh of my flesh.' Sexual intimacy between a man and a woman is the normal method of male/female bonding (emotionally and physically) because it corresponds to the design of our bodies and because it is the normal means by which offspring are created. If God had intended the human race to be fulfilled through both heterosexual and homosexual marriage, He would have designed our bodies to allow reproduction through both means and made both means of sexual intercourse healthy and natural."[35]

ASK YOURSELF

Why did God erect the fence of traditional marriage?

Why do some want it removed?

Why is the design of marriage to be based on what God says rather than on what is said by the government, political activists, or gay-rights groups?

According to James Dobson, what will same-sex marriage, if legalized, lead to?

Elton John and David Furnish adopted a child on December 25, 2010. Do you believe that gay parents can provide for the emotional and spiritual well-being of a child?

Is the movement toward same-sex marriage something that Christians should tolerate or actively renounce?

Suggested reading: *Marriage Under Fire: Why We Must Win This Battle* (James Dobson).

Chapter 5   Burning Lust

"I made a covenant with my eyes not to look lustfully at a girl."—Job 31: 1, NIV.

"Let's not pretend this is easier than it really is. If you want to live a morally pure life, here's what you have to do. You have to blind your right eye the moment you catch it in a lustful leer. You have to choose to live one-eyed or else be dumped on a moral trash pile."—Matthew 5:27–29, The Message.

At this moment [when lust takes control], God...loses all reality....Satan does not fill us with hatred of God, but with forgetfulness of God.[36]—Dietrich Bonhoeffer

Hold not conference, debate, or reasoning with any lust; 'tis but a preparatory for thy admission of it. The way is at the very first flatly to deny it.[37]—Thomas Fuller

Sexual lust may be described as a sexual craving, longing, or desiring. The sources which stir it are people, movies/videos, books, photos, and music from without, and impure memories from within—all spearheaded by the demons of Hell. Lust is manifested when the mind allows sexual imaginations to be entertained (sexual fantasies). These sexual fantasies often find satisfaction in masturbation or lead to fleshing out the desire with another person.

It might be said that lust is the sensual salt that causes a person to thirst for sexual gratification. James states quite bluntly that man "is drawn away of his own lust, and enticed. Then when lust hath conceived, it bringeth forth sin: and sin, when it is finished, bringeth forth death" (James 1:14–15). The word translated "lust" here is *exelkomenos,* which carries the picture of a fish being drawn out of its hiding place (the safety of the deep or the brush pile). The word translated "entice" is *deleazomenos,* which means "to bait, to catch a fish with bait, or to hunt with snares." James thus presents the modus operandi of lust. Satan begets immoral, perverted desires in the heart. If there is a conception, there has to be a father, and in this case it has to be the ruler of darkness. These cravings of sexual desire draw a person from the place of safety with the Lord, only to be "baited" to partake of its forbidden pleasure. Ultimately, lust results in sin, and the sin in death. Some want to blame God, friends, their genes, or circumstances for their sin. This text clearly reveals man's personal responsibility for sin—that it is his own evil desire that prompts it.

Jesus not only forbids immoral sexual activity physically but mentally. He said, "You have heard that it was said, 'You must not be guilty of adultery.' But I tell you that if anyone looks at a woman and wants to sin sexually with her, in his mind he has already done that sin with the woman" (Matthew 5:27–28, NCV). (This is why masturbation is a sin, for it is lust that fuels the act.) In addition to sexual fantasies, lust stimulates and fuels sexual acts forbidden by God, including premarital sex (1 Thessalonians 4:3); adultery (Exodus 20:14); homosexuality (Leviticus 18:22); and sexual rape (Deuteronomy 22:25). Lust soils the soul with sin, steals allegiance from God, stunts growth spiritually, saturates the mind with deviant desires, spoils relationships, sickens the mind and body, sorrows with remorse for its indulgence, shackles with almost unbreakable chains and spurs immoral acts.

Frederick Buechner declared, "Lust is the ape that gibbers in our loins. Tame him as we will by day, he rages all the wilder in our dreams by night. Just when we think we're safe from him, he raises up his ugly head and smirks, and there's no river in the world flows cold and strong enough to strike him down."[38] All can identify with Buechner for none is exempt from the ongoing battle of lust. F. B. Meyer has an interesting illustration regarding lust. "Let me illustrate by the use of botany. You know that flowers have their sex, and the bees gathering honey in one flower carry the pollen to

22

another, and the result is flower and fruit. Precisely in the same way the heart of man is always open, and bees of all kinds seem to bring the pollen of unholy thoughts; when these are sown in the desires of our nature, there is at once the result of which St. James speaks. As soon as you allow the evil thought to mingle with your nature, it bringeth forth the act of sin; and sin, when it is finished, bringeth forth death."[39]

A poem by Shel Silverstein entitled "The Yipiyuk" describes the struggle and defeat that all experience with lust.

In the swamplands long ago,

Where the weeds and mudglumps grow,

A Yipiyuk bit on my toe—

Exactly why I do not know.

I kicked and cried and hollered, "Oh!"

The Yipiyuk would not let go.

I whispered to him soft and low.

The Yipiyuk would not let go.

Yes, that was sixteen years ago,

And the Yipiyuk still won't let go.

The snow may fall; the winds may blow;

The Yipiyuk will not let go.

I drag him 'round each place I go;

And now, my child, at last you know

Exactly why I walk so slow.[40]

The "Yipiyuk" of lust can be overcome, but not without continuous battle. Author John Piper cites six things necessary to defeat lust, listing them in the form of an acronym: A-N-T-H-E-M.

A—AVOID, as much as it is possible and reasonable, the sights and situations that arouse unfitting desire.

N—Say NO to every lustful thought within five seconds. And say it with the authority of Jesus Christ: "In the name of Jesus, NO!"

T—TURN the mind forcefully toward Christ as a superior satisfaction. Saying no will not suffice. You must move from defense to offense. Fight fire with fire. Attack the promises of sin with the promises of Christ.

H—HOLD the promise and the pleasure of Christ firmly in your mind until it pushes the other images out. "Fix your thoughts on Jesus" (Hebrews 3:1, NIV). Here is where many fail. They give in too soon.

E—ENJOY a superior satisfaction. Cultivate the capacities for pleasure in Christ. One reason lust reigns in so many is that Christ has so little appeal to them. We default to deceit because we have little delight in Christ.

M—MOVE into a useful activity away from idleness and other vulnerable behaviors. Lust grows fast in the garden of leisure. Find a good work to do, and do it with all your might.[41]

A Faulkner character was asked his opinion of original sin. He replied, "Well, it's like this. I ain't got to, but I can't help it."[42] He was wrong. The flesh shouts loudly that one can't help lusting, but God clearly states all can be conquerors over the flesh.

The apostle Paul warns us not to sow to the flesh (Galatians 6:8). To sow to the flesh is to stroke it mentally or physically instead of renouncing and crucifying it. A person sows to the flesh by planting its sensual seeds in the mind. Seeds sown that produce lust or acts of physical sexual misconduct include pornography, indecent touches upon the body of another, sensual looks and gazes on another, association with people whose conversation and conduct spark it, and giving place to people or stuff that continuously fuel it. The reason so many fall into sexual sin is that they sow to the flesh, positioning themselves for defeat. The key to defeating lust is to sow to the Spirit—Bible study, prayer, submission to the Holy Spirit's prompting, Scripture memory, godly obedience, worship, moral restraint. In so doing, you will reap the fruit of the Spirit (Galatians 6:8), which is self-control, peace, joy, love, patience, gentleness, faith, meekness and moral goodness (Galatians 5:22–23). In essence, Paul surmises that the secret to victory over the flesh is to give no place to it (Ephesians 4:27), mentally or physically.

ASK YOURSELF

Why is lust a sin?

List several results of lust.

Do you identify with the poem "The Yipiyuk," and, if so, in what way?

The acronym A-N-T-H-E-M spells out the way to victory over lust. What does it stand for?

Will you right now renounce in Jesus' name the place given to lustful imaginations, and hit the delete key, mentally erasing the stored files of pictures, people, and lewd material that have for so long fueled them?

What is the biblical lesson of sowing and reaping?

In what ways is it possible to sow unto the flesh?

What is the modus operandi of lust, according to James?

Memorize and apply to your life 2 Corinthians 10:5, "For the weapons of our warfare are not carnal, but mighty through God to the pulling down of strong holds; Casting down imaginations, and every high thing that exalteth itself against the knowledge of God, and bringing into captivity every thought to the obedience of Christ."

Chapter 6   Is Premarital Sex Always a Sin?

"And it came to pass, as she spake to Joseph day by day, that he hearkened not unto her, to lie by her, or to be with her."—Genesis 39:10.

"Then it happened in the spring, at the time when kings go out to battle, that David..."—2 Samuel 11:1, NASB.

My church group went through the True Love Waits ceremony. At that time, I said I would wait from then on; but on my prom night, I didn't wait. Now I am six months pregnant and alone. The guy didn't stick around.[43]—Jennifer

I have a friend that I really looked up to. He's in the eleventh grade. When I first met him, he was what some would call a Jesus freak. He talked about his relationship with God and how it totally changed the way he lived. He seemed so sincere, so unstoppable, as a believer. But that was last year. This year he got involved in a relationship with a girl that seemed innocent enough at first. Things got serious quickly. She was a Christian too. I mean, what more could you ask for? An attractive girlfriend, a strong relationship with God. I'll never forget the day that I heard the news that she was pregnant and that he left her....I do know that one sexual act changed everything for him. He never comes to church anymore. And I believe his girlfriend got an abortion. So many hurt lives! So many things that they could have avoided if they had just waited.[44]—Geoff

From the outset, I want to answer the question that is posed in the title of the chapter. Without hesitation, I can say that the Bible emphatically says engaging in sexual relations prior to marriage is always a sin (1 Thessalonians 4:3; 1 Corinthians 6: 9–10; 13–20). There are no exception clauses.

E. Stanley Jones, twentieth-century missionary and theologian, stated, "The battle of life as a whole will probably not rise above the sex battle. Lose the sex battle, and defeat spreads into every portion of your being. Win it, and all of life is lifted by that victory."[45] Joseph defeated the temptation of sex with the wife of Potiphar, but, tragically, David faltered when he was tempted by his look at Bathsheba.

Joseph's Keys to Victory over the Sex Temptation

He had his eyes wide open all of the time. Joseph had determined beforehand what his response would be to any temptation to commit adultery. He would absolutely refusal to yield to it. Settle the question long before the temptation ever arises, as Joseph did.

He knew the right words to say. "For her unclean solicitation, he returneth pure and wholesome words."[46] Frankly, Joseph told Potiphar's wife that to engage in such an act would be a great transgression against God (Genesis 39:9–10). In advance of the temptation, determine sure and firm responses to the seductive questions and words that will be used by the tempter to target your heart.

He tried to keep his distance from her. This was not the last time this immoral woman accosted Joseph. He was smart enough to keep some space between them, and the same strategy would be smart of anyone seeking to escape the possibility of moral failure.

He had his feet ready to run at all times. Joseph was on guard against this woman's propositions, and when she actually took hold of his garment one day, he ran from the temptation. You must do the same at times, lest you be overcome and yield (verse 12). "Flee...youthful lusts" (2 Timothy 2:22). When you flee the sex temptation, run into the arms of Jesus in prayer, run to the snack bar, run to the phone, run to a friend, or run somewhere else, but escape it immediately.

He had his heart in the right place. You will never be able to say no to this temptation until, like Joseph, you first say yes to God (verse 2). Cultivate intimacy with Christ through the consistent intake of the Word, prayer, obedience, and lingering in His presence. Joseph confronted his sexual encounter triumphantly, and all of his life was lifted by that victory. The same may be true for you.

David's Moral Failure

"Then it happened in the spring, at the time when kings go out to battle, that David sent Joab and his servants with him and all Israel, and they destroyed the sons of Ammon and besieged Rabbah. But David stayed at Jerusalem.

"Now when evening came David arose from his bed and walked around on the roof of the king's house, and from the roof he saw a woman bathing; and the woman was very beautiful in appearance.

"So David sent and inquired about the woman. And one said, 'Is this not Bathsheba, the daughter of Eliam, the wife of Uriah the Hittite?'

"David sent messengers and took her, and when she came to him, he lay with her; and when she had purified herself from her uncleanness, she returned to her house" (2 Samuel 11:1–4).

The saddest words in the biography of David's life are, "Then it happened." King David, a spiritual giant who penned many Psalms and pursued the very heart of God, in a weak moment dropped his guard and engaged in an act of adultery. This scarlet sin injured not only his life, in that he never again soared as high spiritually, but also the cause of God (2 Samuel 12:14), and the lives of his own children. How tragically sad is this record of David's moral failure!

The church has records of far too many spiritual men like David who, due to undisciplined eyes and unconstrained passion, gave way to their fleshly impulse to engage in an act of illicit sex, damaging their lives and walk with Christ. Even if you are as deeply devoted to God as David was, I caution you with the words of the Apostle Paul: "Let him that thinketh he standeth take heed lest he fall" (1 Corinthians 10:12). You may think that of all the sins you might ever commit, this is one that would not be on the list. Perhaps David thought that. I am sure thousands of ministerial students and ministers down the corridor of history thought that.

And "then it happened." And with its happening came pain, misery, heartache, inescapable guilt, at times pregnancy, and shipwreck of ministry. Oh, how awfully sad it is to hear of a brother or sister in Christ who was spiraling upward toward holiness and an awesome ministry, only to lose it due to an uncontrolled moment of lust!

Keep thy heart with all vigilance, guys! Keep the armor on at all times. Flee youthful lusts. Consider the cost of an immoral sex act before doing it. Learn from David's experience and avoid this moral failure at all costs.

Scripture declares, "The blueness of a wound cleanseth away evil" (Proverbs 20:30). Solomon wisely states here that a stern physical discipline is necessary at times to break away from the most stubborn, enticing and persistent sin.

David repented of this sin and was forgiven (Psalm 51). If you have engaged in immoral sexual activity, you can also be forgiven and restored through Jesus Christ. Don't wait thirteen months to repent and confess this sin, as David did; do it now (1 John 1:7, 9). Avoid the sad words of Scripture regarding a great saint's moral failure that state, "Then it happened." May such words never be written in your biography.

Presently, are you resisting the sex temptation victoriously like Joseph, or have you become vulnerable unto it like David?

ASK YOURSELF

Do you agree with E. Stanley Jones' statement? Why or why not?

Have you had an encounter similar to that of Joseph? If so, did you resist or submit?

How might you handle such an encounter in the future?

What will be your response to a dating partner who solicits sex?

Contrast the manner in which David (2 Samuel 11:2–4) and Joseph faced the sex temptation (Genesis 39:7–13).

Have you made the True Love Pledge to wait until marriage to engage in sex, and, if so, have you kept it?

Chapter 7   Alcohol

"Look not thou upon the wine when it is red, when it giveth his colour in the cup, when it moveth itself aright. At the last it biteth like a serpent, and stingeth like an adder."—Proverbs 23:31–32.

If Satan told you, "I am going to make you into a drunkard, with the loss of all that life holds dear; I will take away your power to hold a job, the love of your wife, the respect of your children, your means of support, your health; I will cause you to be buried in a pauper's grave and wake up in a drunkard's Hell"—I say, if Satan told anyone that, he could never get him to drink. So I beg you in Jesus' name, stop and think! Consider how drink ends before you begin it![47]—John R. Rice

I do not drink alcoholic liquors; I have better use for my head. To put alcohol in the human brain is like putting sand in the bearings of an engine.[48]—Thomas Edison

How often has your attention been drawn to a blinking neon sign bearing the word "Bar"? It is a good name to describe its nature. The intoxicating drink and evil company this establishment offers certainly are bars to respectability, to happiness, to marital fidelity, to domestic felicity, to prosperity, and, ultimately, to Heaven. The commodities of the "Bar" are but roads that lead a person to moral degradation, sorrow, disease, vices of all sorts, poverty, and emptiness.

Dr. Robert Haas, M.D., former president of the American College of Sports Nutrition, said, "Beer, wine, and hard liquor form toxic substances called aldehydes that can destroy the liver, kidney, and brain cells. Aldehydes serve a useful function in preserving or pickling dead animal tissue, but they serve no beneficial purpose in

33

people."[49] The Office of Highway Safety, Madison, Wisconsin, declared, "The most drastic and noticed effect of alcohol is the brain. It depresses brain centers, progressively produces uncoordination, confusion, disorientation, stupor, anesthesia, coma, death. Alcohol kills brain cells, and brain damage is permanent."[50] "Alcohol has adverse effects on your esophagus, stomach and intestines, bloodstream, pancreas, liver, heart, bladder, kidneys, glands, and your brain."[51] Intoxicating beverages seem to give strength but, in reality, cause weakness; seem to create heat but, in fact, lower the body temperature; seem to impart vitality but, in truth, destroy life; seem to promote happiness but generate the greatest unhappiness and misery man can know.[52] Alcohol kills. It is the number-one killer of young people who are under the age of twenty-five in America.

Dr. William Boos, toxicologist, states, "Alcohol is a poison classed among the narcotic drugs, along with chonal, ethyl chloride, chloroform, ether, toluol, and benzol. It acts as poison acts."[53] Dr. Melvin H. Knisely said, "Every time a person takes a few beers or cocktails at a social function, he permanently damages his brain, and probably his heart and liver also."[54] One in ten people who partake of alcohol will become addicted, and, once this occurs, breaking free is extremely difficult.

But what does the Bible say about alcohol consumption? Norman Geisler, former Dean of Liberty Center for Christian Scholarship, Liberty University, has written: "Many wine-drinking Christians today mistakenly assume that what the New Testament meant by wine is identical to wine used today. This, however, is false. In fact, today's wine is, by biblical definition, strong drink and, hence, forbidden by the Bible. What the Bible frequently meant by 'wine' was basically purified water. Therefore, Christians ought not to drink wine, beer, or other alcoholic beverages, for they are actually strong drink forbidden in Scripture. Even ancient pagans did not drink what some Christians drink today."[55] "Wine is a mocker, strong drink is raging: and whosoever is deceived thereby is not wise" (Proverbs 20: 1).

A Biblical Description of Alcohol

"For in the end it bites like a poisonous snake; it stings like a viper."—Proverbs 23:32, NLT.

Alcohol is like the fangs of a snake full of venomous poison awaiting an unsuspecting passer-by. Once alcohol is consumed, its poison is released into the body to do its deadly, destructive work. It kills the brain cells, deadens the senses, retards the reflexes, damages glands and vital organs, and initiates the process of death.

Alcohol is like the robber who steals all one possesses, leaving him in deep poverty. "For the drunkard and the glutton shall come to poverty: and drowsiness shall clothe a man with rags" (Proverbs 23:21). Alcohol is like Mr. Hyde taking over Dr. Jekyll's speech, leading him to say unruly and embarrassing things. "Thine heart shall utter perverse things" (Proverbs 23:33). Alcohol is like a man in the ocean, under its control being tossed to and fro, unaware of what's happening. "Yea, thou shalt be as he that lieth down in the midst of the sea" (Proverbs 23:34). Alcohol is like a mule whose blinders are removed; his eyes are free to roam the terrain (the forbidden), resulting in impure conduct. Alcohol retards mental rationality and deteriorates walls of sexual restraint. "Thine eyes shall behold strange women" (Proverbs 23:33). Alcohol is like a man getting beaten up in a fight, unaware of the harm received; he denies the hurt that alcohol produces in his life. "And you will say, 'They hit me, but I didn't feel it. I didn't even know it when they beat me up'" (Proverbs 23:35, NLT). Alcohol is like the tyrant that enslaves a person to serve him alone; the drunkard can't wait until he sleeps off his intoxication so he can drink again. "When will I wake up so I can look for another drink?" (Proverbs 23:35, NLT). Alcohol is like a pretender—pretending to give a person gusto in life, only to give sorrow. "Wine is a mocker, strong drink is raging: and whosoever is deceived thereby is not wise" (Proverbs 20:1). Alcohol is the mother of sorrows and the father of trouble. "Who has anguish? Who has sorrow? Who is always fighting? Who is always complaining? Who has unnecessary bruises? Who has bloodshot eyes? It is the one who spends long hours in the taverns, trying out new drinks" (Proverbs 23:29–30, NLT).

Additional biblical reasons for abstinence from alcohol include the example principle—be the best representative of the Lord possible (1 Timothy 4:12); the glory principle—engage in conduct that brings glory to God (1 Corinthians 10:31); the Temple principle—the heart is the dwelling place of the Holy Spirit and not to be defiled with sin or damaged by any substance (1 Corinthians 6:19); the sanctification principle—the believer is to be separate from polluting conduct in spite of any trend of the day (Leviticus 20:7); and the weaker brother principle—avoid conduct that will cause a brother to stumble (Romans 14:21).

According to tradition, this is how an Eskimo hunter kills a wolf. First, he coats the blade of a sharp knife with animal blood and allows it to freeze. Next, he adds layer upon layer of animal blood to the blade until the blade is completely concealed with frozen blood. The hunter then places the knife into the snow-covered ground with its blade pointing upward. A wolf, picking up the scent of the blood, locates the knife and licks it faster and faster, harder and harder, until its keen razor sharp edge is bare. His craving for blood masks the sting of the blade cutting into his mouth and the realization that the blood he now is licking is his own. Ultimately, the wolf's carnivorous appetite for more and more blood ends in his own death.

Students turn to alcohol (also to drugs, sex, pornography, gambling, tobacco, and so on) for the same reason the wolf licks the knife blade. It is appealing and appears to be pleasurable and harmless. But soon the law of diminishing returns sets in, requiring more and more of the same to satisfy the desire. Soon it's not one drink, but three drinks that are required; then it is not three drinks, but a case. Faster and harder one licks the deceptive bait blade of alcohol until a crisis develops, or even death. The wolf didn't see the result that was coming, nor do those who take that first drink and second drink and...It's just the baiting scheme Satan uses to lure one into a snare, only then to destroy body, mind, and soul. The law of sowing and reaping applies not only to seed planted in the soil, but also in the heart (Galatians 6:7). This law clearly teaches that a person may choose the seed he plants in the sod of the soul, but he cannot choose its outcome. A person always reaps what is sown, whether the harvest is desired or detested.

Alexander the Great is an example of this spiritual law. He was ruler of Macedonia at age sixteen, a victorious general at age eighteen, and a king at age twenty, only to die as a drunkard before the age of thirty-three. On a second night of partying with twenty guests in Babylon, he drank to the health of all at the table. Next, he took the huge capacity of Hercules' cup full of alcohol and drank all of it to Proteas, a Macedonian who was present. Filling the cup once again, Alexander drank to himself and instantly fell to the floor. A few days later, he was dead. He who conquered the then known world failed to master himself.[56] Regarding Alexander the Great and every young person whose life is cut short or squandered due to alcohol consumption, I cannot help but think of John Greenleaf Whittier's poetic words: "For of all sad words of tongue or pen, the saddest are these: 'It might have been!'"[57]

The effects of alcohol upon the mind, upon the body, upon others, and upon one's testimony should be more than enough cause for abstinence from alcohol. Deliverance from the addictive grip of alcohol is impossible apart from divine intervention, relentless resolve, loving support from friends and family, and counseling. The surest safeguard against alcohol addiction and the hell it brings into one's life is not taking a first drink. Billy Graham declared, "It is my judgment that because of the devastating problem that alcoholism has become in America, it is better for Christians to be teetotalers, except for medicinal purposes."[58]

ASK YOURSELF

What might be your response to another who states, "Drinking in moderation is okay"?

Do you know of someone whose life was devastated or destroyed by alcohol?

How would you reason with another about the perils of drinking, seeking their abstinence?

Is there any harm socializing with those who drink (dates, parties, and bars)? Why or why not?

How does Solomon compare one who consumes alcohol to one bitten by a poisonous snake, to one adrift in the ocean, to one beaten up in a fight, and to a pretender?

How does alcohol lead to sexual immorality?

If you were to sum up Solomon's council regarding strong drink, what would you state? Why?

Relate the illustration of the wolf and make application.

[For help, contact your pastor/student minister or call 1-800-999-9999 (Covenant House)]

Chapter 8   Drugs: Heroes to Zeros

"But test everything that is said. Hold on to what is good. Stay away from every kind of evil."—1 Thessalonians 5:21–22, NLT.

Many young people turn to drugs in an effort to escape from their problems, but drugs are not an escape; they're a trap. "Come to me," Jesus says to the person who seeks relief through drugs, and "I will give you rest" (Matthew 11:28). While drugs is a complex addiction and challenging problem, it can be best pre-vented—and overcome—with the power of God through life in the Spirit.[59]—Josh McDowell

Nikki Sixx, band leader for Mötley Crüe, hit bottom due to alcohol, drugs, and sex. Heroin addiction led to his death, but two shots of adrenaline to his heart revived him. Nikki testified that due to his lifestyle, the popular band went from being "big heroes to being zeros."[60] No doubt, all who have walked in Nikki's shoes of drug abuse can attest to the same—that drug usage takes you farther than you want to go, costs you more than you want to pay, and keeps you longer than you want to stay.

Drugs disarm the will

The inhibitions are drastically lowered under the influence of drugs, resulting in sexual acts in which one in his sane mind would never engage, acts of violence, crime, self-mutilation, and even murder. A "young man under the influence of 'angel dust' peeled his face from his skull with pieces of a mirror and fed the flesh to his pet dogs."[61] More than a third (36%) of sexually active young people aged 15 to 24 say that alcohol or drugs have influenced their decisions about sex, including more than a quarter

39

(29%) who say they have "'done more"' sexually than they had planned to do while drinking or using drugs.[62] It's really a scary deal to put the control panel of life in the hands of some drug.

Drugs dominate the mind

Gradually, usage of a drug lessens the "rush" received, pressing the user to seek out a stronger dosage or a heavier substance. How do such addicts feel?

"Addicts feel as if they are trapped and out of control. They feel like abject worshippers, devoted to something that can be very dangerous. They feel desperate hunger and thirst for something. They feel like they can't let go, clinging even when the addictive behavior yields very few pleasures and a great deal of pain. They feel like they are in bondage. Addicts feel out of control, enslaved, stuck, and without hope for freedom or escape. Something other than the living God controls them, and the controlling object tells them how to live, think, and feel."[63]

A casual viewing of the television documentary "Intervention" well pictures this truth. Students dominated, controlled by a chemical substance will stop at almost nothing to satisfy their drug craving. One student in dire straits for a fix killed his parents to acquire money to purchase what was needed for a "rush."

Drugs destroy the life

It is undeniable and obvious that drugs rob from a person his purpose in life, self-esteem, peace, hope, healthy relationships, sane mind (emotional trauma), academic achievement potential, health, and perhaps life (by suicide, overdose, accident, or murder).

Drugs damage others

The drug user not only jeopardizes his life, but he endangers that of others. The list of possible harmful effects the drug user poses to others includes assault, birth defects, unsafe sex, acts of violence, murder, and injury or death as a result of driving under the influence of a drug. The drug abuser further injures his testimony (if he is a Christian) and is a stumbling block for others to be saved.

Drug abstinence is clearly the biblical standard. "But test everything that is said. Hold on to what is good. Stay away from every kind of evil" (1 Thessalonians 5:21–22, NLT).

"[Evil] is always to be understood in the active sense as denoting something malignant, working mischief, hurting all with whom it comes into contact. Who, then, would want to have contact with such a thing in any form? It blasts, poisons, kills. Keep away from it entirely. We should not restrict this command to the field of morals. The worst forms of wickedness consist of perversion of the truth, of spiritual lies, although today many look upon these forms with indifference and regard them rather harmless. The fact that moral perversions are included is self-evident; these also work to destroy the spiritual life and appear in many forms."[64]

Drugs do make a person feel, as Nikki Sixx said, like a zero. But God specializes in taking nobodies and transforming them into somebodies. Christ who died on a cross for failures stands ready to receive and forgive you this very moment. "Christ receiveth sinful men, even me with all my sin."

ASK YOURSELF

What are the dangers of substance abuse to a person personally?

Describe how one addicted to drugs might feel.

If the user is a professing believer, what additional impact on his life do drugs yield?

What dangers does the drug user pose to others?

What is the biblical standard regarding drug usage?

What steps must be taken for the drug abuser to be set free from the tyrant of drugs?

[Contact your pastor/student minister or call 1-800-999-9999 (Covenant House) for help]

9   Gambling

"But those who desire to be rich fall into temptation, into a snare, into many senseless and harmful desires that plunge people into ruin and destruction. For the love of money is a root of all kinds of evils. It is through this craving that some have wandered away from the faith and pierced themselves with many pangs."—1 Timothy 6:9–10, ESV.

The paradox with gambling is that if you win, you lose. If you lose, you lose. If you win, the high consumes your mind until you're back in action. If you lose, you crash and chase your losses to regain that high.[65]—Gambling addict

Every night that I finished gambling, I'd say, "That's it. I'm not going to do this anymore. It's gotta stop." And the next day, I'd be gambling again.[66]—Gambling addict

What is gambling? John MacArthur stated, "Gambling is an activity in which a person risks something of value, usually money. It's an activity in which a person risks something of value to forces of chance completely beyond his control or any rational expectation. That's it. It is an activity in which a person risks something of value to forces of chance completely beyond his control or any rational expectation in hope of winning something of greater value, usually more money. But it is an appeal to sheer chance."[67]

Gambling is like smoking and pornography in that it is not specifically named in the Bible but is nevertheless condemned, along with them, through principles and precepts that are set forth in passages like the following ones.

Proverbs 29:19–22
Proverbs 13:11
1 Timothy 6:6–11
1 Timothy 5:8
Exodus 20:17

Although the legal age for gambling is over eighteen, there are still many teens who pawn possessions, borrow money, steal, prostitute themselves, falsely use credit cards, and lie so that they can obtain the money with which to gamble. The Internet has opened wide the door for teens to gamble. An estimated 5.7 million teens are classified as problem gamblers, and an additional 2.2 million are considered pathological or compulsive gamblers, making a total of 7.9 million teens who are strongly impacted by a desire to gamble.[68]

Whether or not a person is classified as a problem gambler is not determined by how often he gambles or by the amount of money he loses, but by the extent of disruption in his life caused by this habit; i.e., the use of money for gambling that was designated for a car payment or a tuition payment, sleep deprivation due to staying up too late gambling on the Internet or in a club, failing grades or missed classes in school, or injury to personal relationships.

The American Psychiatric Association uses certain criteria to identify pathological gamblers. "The three cardinal signs of PG are (1) preoccupation with gambling and obtaining money with which to gamble; (2) loss of control of one's gambling; that is, not following reasonable limits of time and money spent on gambling; and (3) continuation of gambling despite adverse consequences, such as continuing to gamble in spite of losing large sums of money."[69] However, the term problem gambling is a general term used for both categories.

Consequences of teen gambling addictions include declining grades, habitual money problems, less time for friends and family, and temptation to engage in illegal behavior to get money to pay off gambling debts—leading to possible jail time and associations with unsavory characters who could make life difficult if they are not paid.[70] This addiction takes priority over friends, family, classes, and God. It often leads to severe desperation for a way out and depression that leads to suicide. Among the most salient risk factors with gambling are substance use, abuse, and dependence. The link between gambling and alcohol, illicit drugs, and tobacco use is strong.[71]

Do you or a friend have a problem with gambling? If you would have to answer yes to any one of the following questions, that would reveal a gambling addiction.[72]

1. Have you often gambled longer than you had planned to?

2. Have you often gambled until your last dollar was gone?

3. Have thoughts of gambling caused you to lose sleep?

4. Have you used your income or savings to gamble while letting bills go unpaid?

5. Have you made repeated, unsuccessful attempts to stop gambling?

6. Have you broken the law or considered breaking the law to finance your gambling?

7. Have you borrowed money to finance your gambling?

8. Have you felt depressed or suicidal because of your gambling losses?

9. Have you been remorseful after gambling?

10. Have you gambled to get money to meet your financial obligations?

Additional indicators that identify a problem with gambling are tolerance (a need for higher or more frequent wagers to obtain the same "rush"); irritability or restlessness in any attempt to stop; chasing (the need to try to win back losses); bailout (looks to family and others for money to bail out of gambling losses); loss of control (unsuccessful in reducing or stopping gambling); lying (to hide the problem or the extent of it); escape (to improve moods or to escape problems).[73]

If any of these indicators reveal that you have a personal addiction to gambling, it is imperative that you admit to yourself that you have such a problem. Don't rationalize the truth away. Pretending that you don't have a gambling problem only allows the problem to get worse. As with any wrong, injurious habit or addiction, the first step to freedom is acknowledging a problem exists.

Next, turn to God for deliverance, acknowledging the sin of gambling and pleading for His intervention. God loves you and stands ready to cleanse and liberate.

Third, confide in your parents, student minister, pastor, and/or Christian counselor about this problem and seek their support in attempting to remain free from its clutches. You will need godly people to help you in defeating this enslaving habit, so do not hesitate to ask them for their support. The National Coalition on Problem Gambling at 1-800-522-4700 also stands ready to assist you. Also, you should saturate your mind by taking in megadoses of the Word of God, praying much, and relying upon Him day by day for victory.

Fourth, it is expedient at the outset to let another person manage your money. Paychecks or allowances ought to be regulated by a parent who pays your bills and gives you only what is required for each day's needs.

Fifth, let it be a firm and standing rule that you always avoid places and people that would be a stumbling block in your recovery. The road to recovery starts here and now. It is time to change and be free.

ASK YOURSELF

What is gambling, according to John MacArthur's definition?

Why is gambling a sin?

Contrast the problem gambler with the pathological gambler.

Without looking back, cite five indicators that reveal a person is a problem gambler.

Do you gamble or know others who do?

What are the short and long term consequences of gambling?

How can a person be set free from the gambling trap?

10   Cigarettes

"What? know ye not that your body is the temple of the Holy Ghost which is in you, which ye have of God, and ye are not your own?"—1 Corinthians 6:19.

Cigarettes are killers that travel in packs.[74]

According to the Surgeon General, quitting smoking is the single most important step a smoker can take to improve the length and quality of his or her life.[75]

Statistics show that seventy percent of smokers want to quit and that forty percent make a serious attempt to quit each year; however, each year fewer than five percent of them succeed in quitting permanently. Because nicotine is addictive, most people who want to quit smoking find themselves unable or unwilling to quit when they try.[76]

A good reason why you should not smoke is that *smoking damages the health and leads to premature death*. The Surgeon General of the United States has ordered that every pack of cigarettes bear an inscription stating, "Cigarettes have been found to be hazardous to your health."

Eighty-seven percent of lung cancer deaths are linked to smoking.[77] Research also indicates that smoking doubles a person's risk of heart attack.[78] "Of every 100,000 fifteen-year-old smokers, tobacco will prematurely kill at least 20,000 before the age of seventy."[79] "Each year, smoking kills more people than AIDS, alcohol, drug abuse, car crashes, murders, suicides, and fires—combined. Cigarette smokers die younger than nonsmokers. In fact, smoking decreases a person's life expectancy by ten to twelve years. Smokers between the ages of thirty-five and seventy have death rates three times higher than those who have never smoked."[80] Additionally, smoking is injurious to others who inhale the smoke from the cigarette in a second-hand manner.

The "American Cancer Society, 2000 Report" stated that people who quit smoking, regardless of age, live longer than those who continue to do so. Smokers who quit before age fifty have half the risk of dying in the next fifteen years compared with those who continue to smoke. Quitting smoking substantially decreases the risk of lung, laryngeal, esophageal, oral, pancreatic, bladder, and cervical cancer. Quitting lowers the risk for other major diseases, including coronary heart disease and cardio vascular disease. The Surgeon General of the United States, in a 2011 television advertisement against smoking, stated that when a cigarette is smoked, it releases over 7,000 chemicals, which spread throughout the body.

When cigarettes are burned, the ingredients and additives in them create toxic compounds. There are over 4,000 chemicals in cigarette smoke, more than forty of which are known carcinogens.

Tar—the same thing that is used to pave driveways
Hydrogen cyanide—the chemical used to kill rats
Benzene—which is used in manufacturing gasoline
Acetone—a main ingredient in nail polish remover
Formaldehyde—a substance used as a preservative for dead bodies, as an industrial fungicide, as a disinfectant, and in glues and adhesives
Ammonia—a chemical found in house cleansers
Carbon monoxide—a poison in car exhaust
Nicotine—the drug that is responsible for addiction.[81]

What disgusting and harmful stuff is inhaled with each cigarette smoked!

Smoking is an expensive habit. This is clear when you multiply the cost per pack times the number of packs smoked in a week and then multiply that times the number of years smoking. It is an unattractive habit which yellows the teeth and saturates the clothes and hair with the smell of tobacco. It is also a killing habit, since each cigarette takes eleven minutes off of one's life.[82]

And, of course, it is an addictive habit—most adults who smoke began during their teen years, and, although only five percent of students said they would continue to smoke, seventy-five percent were still smoking seven to nine years later.[83]

Oh, just in case you're interested, the majority of your classmates desire to date a nonsmoker. In light of these truths, why in the world would you want to light up?

Smoking damages the body, which belongs to God, and shortchanges His divine design for it. "Bullets, guns, gas, electric chair, drowning, and hanging are faster; but for slow suicide, there is nothing like cigarettes, cigars, and pipes."[84]

ASK YOURSELF

Name the chemical ingredients or additives found in cigarettes?

Is there any doubt in your mind that cigarette smoking is harmful to the body?

Anyone who smokes, thinking that it is possible to quit at any moment, is deceived. If you smoke and doubt this, you can see its addictive hold on you by trying to go a week without lighting up.

In addition to cancer and heart disease, what are the downsides to smoking?

What is the biblical perspective regarding smoking?

For guidance in quitting smoking, see the principles regarding alcohol listed on page 36 and adapt them to this problem.

11   Smokeless Tobacco

"What? know ye not that your body is the temple of the Holy Ghost which is in you, which ye have of God, and ye are not your own? For ye are bought with a price: therefore glorify God in your body, and in your spirit, which are God's." —1 Corinthians 6:19–20.

Advertising implies that smokeless tobacco habits are innocuous and safe. They are not. Smokeless tobacco products have shown potential for causing cancer of the oral cavity, pharynx, larynx, and esophagus. Smokeless tobacco can produce significant effects on the soft and hard tissues of the mouth, including bad breath, discolored teeth and restorations, excessive wear (abrasion) of the incisal and occlusal surfaces of the teeth, decreased ability to taste and smell, gingival recession, advanced periodontal destruction of the soft and hard tissues, erythema of the soft tissues, leukoplakia, and cancer.[85] —Journal American Dental Association

Bill Tuttle, outfielder for the Detroit Tigers, the Kansas City Athletics, and the Minnesota Twins chewed tobacco for most of his career. More than thirty years after he left baseball, he developed a large tumor in his cheek—so huge that it actually penetrated the cheek and extended through the skin. Surgery was performed which resulted not only in the removal of the tumor but much of Tuttle's face. Youthful usage of chewing tobacco cost him his jawbone, his right cheekbone, many teeth, his gumline, his taste buds, and ultimately his life in 1998. Prior to his death, Tuttle sought to steer youth and others away from smokeless tobacco.[86] Tuttle is testimony to the fact that *smokeless is not harmless* when it comes to tobacco.

The use of chewing tobacco and snuff among students is accelerating. Stained teeth, bad breath, gum recession, and poor dental health are the obvious effects of its consumption; but it, like smoking, may also cause cancer. Smokeless tobacco contains at least twenty-eight cancer-causing chemicals which increase the chance of cancer in the mouth, throat, esophagus and pancreas.[87] Cancer-causing substances in smokeless tobacco include formaldehyde, acetaldehyde, crotonaldehyde, hydrazine, arsenic, nickel, cadmium, benzopyrene, and polonium—which gives off radiation.[88]

Look this stuff up in your chemistry book to understand exactly what poison the smokeless tobacco user ingests. Fifty percent of smokeless tobacco users will develop precancerous patches called leukoplakia within three years of beginning use.[89] Smokeless tobacco clearly is not the harmless alternative to smoking that it is portrayed to be.

Like cigarettes, smokeless tobacco contains the highly addictive drug nicotine. Nicotine revs up the mind, producing pleasurable feelings; but once the kick wears off, it causes many smokeless tobacco users to feel tired, depressed, and down. In order to feel the high again, they have to partake of more of the substance, creating an endless cycle of ups and downs. The addictive power of nicotine is so strong that of the thirty-five million tobacco users who try to quit annually, only one out of fifteen actually succeed for more than a month.[90]

A tobacco company salesman stated, "Once a kid's hooked, he doesn't leave." Research bears him out, for it reveals that of all the habits one acquires in adolescence, chewing tobacco is the one that is most likely to stick with him the rest of his life. Seriously consider the health facts about smokeless tobacco and allow them to supersede the pressure or other motivations you may encounter to consume the substance. Your best for the future warrants it.

As a Christian, your body is the Temple of God; and avoidance of any substance that disgraces, damages, or destroys it is commanded by God (1 Corinthians 6:19–20).

ASK YOURSELF

In exchange for the temporary pleasure of smokeless tobacco, what will I receive in years to come?

Is smokeless tobacco the safe alternative to smoking?

If you are a user, have you ever tried to quit?

What would you advise a friend to do if he was considering the consumption of smokeless tobacco?

As a Christian, list several reasons why you shouldn't partake of this substance.

For guidance in quitting the use of smokeless tobacco, see the principles regarding alcohol listed on page 36 and adapt them to this problem.

12   Music

"It is better to hear the rebuke of the wise, than for a man to hear the song of fools." —Ecclesiastes 7:5.

You can hypnotize people with the music, and then, when you get them at their weakest point, you can preach into their subconscious what you want to say.[91]—Jimmy Hendrix

David Bowie, while in his prime as a rock musician, frankly said, "Rock has always been the Devil's music....I believe rock and roll is dangerous....I feel we're only heralding something even darker than ourselves."[92]

I agree with Bowie's assessment. Much of today's rock music is a herald of darkness and therefore potentially dangerous to its audience. It is a purveyor of darkness. It is dangerous, in that it exalts Satan; exploits sex; endorses drugs and alcohol; distorts the truth; encourages pornography; embraces homosexuality; excites suicide; elicits rebellion to authority such as parents, police, and teachers; espouses violence; and effects an influence on the mind by altering convictions, philosophy, and standards of life.

Alan Bloom, writing of the impact of rock music on the average teenager, states, "It is their passion; nothing else excites them as it does; they cannot take seriously anything alien to music."[93]

According to a report on rock music by Light Youth Ministries, a person with rock music in his or her life has in the subconscious mind an influence that will cancel all the normal power of the work of the Word of God.[94]

57

Knowing this, students must no longer look at rock music as mere harmless entertainment, but as a medium that can destroy their faith and dilute biblical values that have been ingrained into their lives.

The Christian should not listen to music that slaps God in the face, whether it is rock music, country music, or any other currently popular genre. He should not choose music whose artist is the advocate of Satan in regards to how a person should live. He must avoid music that undermines Christian values or that is a hindrance to spiritual intimacy with Almighty God.

The Bible sets forth a universal principle that must be applied to what the Christian sees, where he goes, what he does, what he thinks, what he says, and, yes, to what he hears. This principle, found in 1 Corinthians 10:31, states, "So whether you eat or drink, or whatever you do, do it all for the glory of God," NLT.

That's a pretty dogmatic statement to make, isn't it? Ask yourself this list of questions.

"Does God receive honor when I listen to rock music?"

"Can I glorify Him by choosing to listen to this music?"

"Is the music to which I listen consistent with biblical doctrine and scriptural principles?"

"Is the artist to whom I am listening trying to push views of darkness upon me?"

"Are the artist's moral and religious beliefs consistent with the Bible?"

If music to which you are listening passes this acid test, then freely listen to it and enjoy it. However, if the music you choose for your entertainment cannot be considered suitable for a Christian in the light of these questions, it would be better for you and more pleasing to God if you would change to another radio station and/or discard the CD from which you are hearing the music.

ASK YOURSELF

Based upon the statistic that students listen to six hours of rock music daily, how important is it to be alert to its potential impact?

If a person is what he eats, he is even more what he hears. Explain.

What possible negative impact could rock music have in your life?

Have you noticed one's clothing, attitude, or lifestyle to be influenced by rock music? If so, in what way?

What actions will you take in the light of the truth presented about rock music?

What listening alternatives to rock music are available to you?

Do you agree or disagree with Alan Bloom's statement regarding the impact of rock music? Why or why not?

13   Suicide: The Preventable Death

"Cast thy burden upon the LORD, and he shall sustain thee."—Psalm 55: 22.

When one door closes, another opens; but we often look so long and so regretfully upon the closed door that we do not see the one which has opened for us.[95]—Alexander Graham Bell

When we long for life without difficulties, remind us that oaks grow strong in contrary winds and diamonds are made under pressure.[96]—Peter Marshall

One of the leading causes of death among students between the ages of fifteen and twenty-four is suicide. In 2008, the Boys Town Hotline (1-800-448-3000) assisted over eleven thousand callers who were thinking about suicide or who had already made the attempt. It is possible that you, just like Boys Town, may have the opportunity to intervene in a friend's suicidal plans, thus saving his or her life.

First, learn to recognize the signs of suicidal tendencies.

These include expressing thoughts of despair, suicide, or death; giving away prized possessions; making a will; making other preparations for death; a change in sleeping patterns, like sleeping too much or sleeping too little; a change in eating habits, leading to losing or gaining more than a little weight; a change in school performance, like suddenly getting poor grades; cutting class; dropping out of school activities; a change in social activities; dropping friends; spending more and more time alone; personality changes; nervousness, agitation, or bursts of anger—or, on the other hand, apathy or carelessness about health and appearance; abuse of alcohol or drugs or other self-destructive behavior, such as getting into a lot of accidents or taking life-risking chances; physical symptoms often related to stress, such as chronic stomachaches, headaches, or fatigue; and previous suicide attempt(s).[97] These signs often appear in clusters.

Second, differentiate fable from fact regarding suicide.

It is a fact, not a fable, that people who talk about suicide are serious. Eight out of ten people who commit suicide speak of it prior to making the attempt.

It is a fact, not a fable, that the chances of suicide are reduced when a person can talk about it.

It is a fact, not a fable, that there are telltale signs such as those cited above which a person exhibits when he or she is considering suicide.

It is a fact, not a fable, that the suicide risk remains in effect even after the crisis that precipitated the original thoughts is over.

It is a fact, not a fable, that the suicidal are undecided about wanting to live or die and that they are gambling that someone will intervene to stop them. Individuals who are stopped in their suicide attempt rarely complain about it.

It is a fact, not a fable, that people just like you can intervene and prevent the suicidal death of a friend or classmate.[98]

Third, prayerfully intervene.

As noted, the person considering suicide wants someone to intervene. If we hesitate in confronting such a person, it may result in our taking action too late. Intervention is warranted whenever there is evidence of a cluster of any of the suicidal signs that were previously listed. Mary Miller is a suicidologist. She suggests that once you know a person intends to take his or her life, you should seek to obtain the answers to four questions that can be remembered through the acronym S-L-A-P.

S—How **S**pecific are the person's plans?

L—How **L**ethal is the proposed method?

A—What is its **A**vailability?

P—What is the **P**roximity of helpful resources like friends or family?[99]

Answers to these questions reveal how serious a stage the suicidal person is in.

Dr. Timothy Faulk, clinical psychological therapist, stated, "Remember that people who are feeling suicidal isolate themselves, so it is vital that we reach out to them. They need you to encourage them to talk, and then they need you to listen carefully. Talk openly and directly about suicide. Use the words 'suicide,' 'kill yourself,' and 'dead' in a matter-of-fact way."[100] Faulk continues, "Be nonjudgmental and accept the person's feelings, even if you disagree with them. Show your interest and support. Don't let the person swear you to secrecy. As a person tells you that he or she is thinking about suicide, start thinking about people you can ask for help [ministers, school counselors, teachers, mental health professionals, and psychologists]. You can do a lot to help the person initially, but the situation is too dangerous to handle entirely on your own."[101]

Never hesitate to call for help in dealing with the suicidal. At the outset, encourage the person who is suicidal to call the suicide hotline and let them know that their identity will not need to be revealed. Numbers they can call are 1-800-SUICIDE or Billy Graham Ministries, 877-247-2426.

Following the suicide of a friend or family member, several stages are normally experienced.

First, there is the initial shock and disbelief of the suicide. This is the intense emotional impact that leaves you feeling as if you are paralyzed. A certain amount of denial takes place as you try to deal with the act of suicide.

Then there is the release of emotions. Normally, this will involve an intense period of weeping as well as a time of sharing about all of the "good" things that the person who committed suicide had done.

Third, there is a period of depression and/or loneliness. The level of depression you experience will depend upon the type of association you had with the deceased person. One common response is to make it seem that the deceased one was closer to you than they actually were. The only thing wrong with this type of thinking is that it tends to lead to extremely unrealistic actions and thoughts.

Next there is often a period of guilt. You find yourself thinking things like *I should have listened to him,* or *I should have been a better friend*, or *It's my fault!* Again, this type of thinking only lends itself to unrealistic thoughts and actions.

Fifth, you are likely to experience hostility and anger. You might think *How could she do such a stupid thing?* or *Why did he do this to us?* or *What did I do wrong as a parent?* or *I thought he was my friend!* You may feel guilty for being angry with someone who is no longer alive, but possibly even more you feel guilty and angry with yourself for allowing the suicide to occur.

A period of hopelessness comes next. You could say things like, "I can't go on without..." or "I couldn't care less," or "Show me where I can find hope, if you can."

This is followed by a slow return of hope. You tell yourself *Life will go on,* or *I will be able to cope.*

Finally, there is the return to normality and reality. This is accomplished by admitting the loss and adjusting to it while drawing strength from God, His promises and His people. God knows how to heal broken hearts![102]

ASK YOURSELF

Are you aware of anyone who is suicidal?

Have you entertained thoughts of suicide?

Differentiating facts from fables, which were eye-openers?

What is your game plan in suicidal intervention?

Who would be your go-to person (student minister, pastor, teacher, etc.) for immediate assistance in coping with a friend's thoughts about suicide?

Is it right to break a confidence to save a friend from suicide?

14   Coping with Suicidal Thoughts

"The thief's purpose is to steal and kill and destroy. My purpose is to give them a rich and satisfying life." —John 10:10, NLT.

God thinks we're worth loving; God thinks we're worth honoring; God thinks we're worth making a sacrifice for; God thinks we're worth providing for; God thinks we're worth planning for; God thinks we're worth delighting in.[103] —David A. Semands

Don't buy into the lie of Satan that you cannot get beyond a broken relationship, difficulty, failure, or the results of wrong conduct. A professor asked an African-American pastor, "What is your favorite verse in Scripture?"

He replied, "And it came to pass."

The professor said, "That's not a verse of Scripture. It is only part of a verse."

The pastor countered, "I know. I have lots of troubles and trials at times, but they all come to pass."

Whatever problems you encounter will "come to pass," even those that are seemingly insurmountable. Troubles and failures are part and parcel of growing up. All have known the depression and pain fueled by guilt and shame you now manifest. The path on which you now walk, others have tread victoriously by looking beyond the moment to the future, holding onto the promise of God that He will neither forsake nor fail them (Hebrews 13:5). Students who sat where you now sit are living highly productive and happy lives—many married with children living the American dream—because they refused to allow the intense pain of the moment to trigger self-destruction.

You will get through this ordeal; the pain will end—I promise. Others have, and you will too. Delay a decision about suicide for a week; give yourself time to clear your head to think rationally. A high school friend killed himself immediately following a break-up with his girlfriend. Had he taken time to clear his head, the decision would have been different.

Don't cross bridges you don't need to cross. Experience has taught me that Satan will have you crossing bridges mentally that never have to be crossed at all. Don't expect friends to fully understand or take your suicidal thoughts seriously to the point of intervention, and don't misread their failure to intervene as indicating unconcern or lack of love. They just don't know how to respond. Talk out your intentions with a student minister, pastor, or another trained counselor. If you prefer, your name need not be shared (National Suicide Prevention Lifeline at 1-800-273-8255; Covenant House NineLine, 1-800-999-9999). Above all, look to God for grace to cope with the pain. Lean heavily upon His unchanging love and promises. God can do anything but fail you. He stands ever ready to initiate a fresh start.

> "I wish that there were some wonderful place
> In the Land of Beginning Again,
> Where all our mistakes and all our heartaches
> And all of our poor selfish grief
> Could be dropped like a shabby old coat at the door
> And never put on again."
> —Louisa Fletcher Tarkington

In the classic poem "The Land of Beginning Again," the writer longs for a land where she can lay aside the past, much as a man puts aside soiled clothes to start fresh. Although in the poem this "Land of Beginning Again" is make-believe, for Christians there is such a place found in a personal relationship with Jesus Christ.

The Bible calls the refreshing new beginning the new birth. This spiritual birth requires "repentance...and faith" (Acts 20:21). You can enter this land of beginning again right now by expressing sorrow to God over sin and desire to turn from it to live for Christ Jesus alone. He is the only one who can erase the past of its guilt and horrors, filling the heart with peace and joy—the only one who can cleanse of sin making man right with God. Right now, make the U-turn to Christ.

A former world chess champion visited a famous art gallery to view a picture of a chess match. The artist depicted a young man seated despairingly at a chessboard in a match against the Devil whose face glowed with a look of malicious triumph. The painting was simply entitled, "Checkmated." The former champion looked intently upon the picture, studying the position of the chess pieces. Suddenly, with a loud voice that rang through the art gallery, he said, "Bring me a chessboard. I can save him yet." The mastermind chess champion had discovered the way out of the Devil's supposed checkmate.

It may appear the Devil has you checkmated with no way out, but Jesus Christ the Champion can give victory if you call upon Him. With Jesus, there is always a way out.

"Humpty Dumpty sat on a wall;
Humpty Dumpty had a great fall.
All the king's horses and all the king's men
Couldn't put Humpty together again."[104]

Regardless of the "fall" experienced—the brokenness of dreams or relationships, or the loss of hope or significance for existing—King Jesus can do what "all the king's horses and all the king's men" cannot do and put you back together again!

ASK YOURSELF

Whether suicidal thoughts just occurred once or they are a recurring thing, don't be embarrassed to seek therapy from a pastor, Christian counselor, or psychologist. As the body needs help from a doctor when it is sick, so the mind needs help from a qualified person when it is depressed. Will you make that call now for help? God's best yet awaits you; don't shortchange yourself and others by committing suicide.

15   Facing the Dark Night of the Soul

"Be strong and of a good courage, fear not, nor be afraid of them: for the LORD *thy God, he it is that doth go with thee; he will not fail thee, nor forsake thee."*—Deuteronomy 31:6.

In no passage of the holy canonical books can there be found either divine precept or permission to take away our own life, whether for the sake of entering on the enjoyment of immortality, or of shunning or ridding ourselves of anything whatever. Nay, the law, rightly interpreted, even prohibits suicide where it says, "Thou shalt not kill."[105]—Augustine

Suicide is not the solution to agonizing emotional pain. It's not a sedative like drugs or alcohol that numbs the pain; it is death to life forever. Every suicide is a mad rush to end unbearable pain without thought to its ultimate end of permanent separation from family and friends.

Life is difficult. It always will be difficult. Part and parcel of growing up are certain heartaches, sorrows, failures, disappointments and frustrations, from which none are exempt. While I was a college student, I heard a chapel speaker say something I have never forgotten, something I hope you will etch upon the walls of your mind. He simply said, "There's a tolerable solution for every intolerable problem you face."

I have proved that statement to be true time and time again. Life is hard, but God is good. He promises to walk through every storm, sorrow, bitter disappointment, lonely moment, and failure with you. He can do anything but fail you. Therefore, fear not that which happens to you or around you, relying upon Him who will not "fail thee, nor forsake thee."

Days of emotional and physical upheaval will come, but they will *pass.* The darkness eventually must give way to the light. God promises to still the boisterous winds and waves beating upon the vessel of your life, saying, "Peace, be still" (Mark 4:39).

Don't panic. Wait on Him. Trust in Him. Soon the raging sea will become as a pane of glass, and tranquility will reign again. "In his favour is life: weeping may endure for a night, but joy cometh in the morning" (Psalm 30:5).

I asked three students if they wanted a twenty-dollar bill which I held in my hand. They all did. I then took the bill, crushed it up in my hands, and again asked who wanted it. Again all responded in the affirmative. Next, tossing the bill onto the floor, I squashed it with my shoe. With the bill in my hand, I then inquired again who still wanted it; no one said they didn't. "Why do you still want this crushed up, wrinkled up, and soiled bill?" I asked.

A twelve year old girl answered, "Because it hasn't lost its value." Wow—what a good answer! Despite the condition of the twenty dollar bill, it had not lost its value. Its blemishes had not altered its worth.

Your life is like the twenty-dollar bill. Your value to God is not based upon what happens to you, but upon the fact that He made you in His own image. You will never depreciate in value to God. He cannot love you any more or any less then He does now. God will love you when you're up and when you're down, when you're in or when you're out, when you're soaring high spiritually or when you have a crash.

Never forget that God's love is not dependent upon performance or popularity or great intellect. It is an unconditional love. No yardstick can measure it. This awesome love cannot be fully described or defined, just accepted and experienced.

This is why the apostle Paul said, "And may you have the power to understand, as all God's people should, how wide, how long, how high, and how deep his love is. May you experience the love of Christ, though it is too great to understand fully. Then you will be made complete with all the fullness of life and power that comes from God" (Ephesians 3:18–19, NLT).

ASK YOURSELF

How do you handle the wrenching pain of a broken relationship, a busted dream, disappointment in a friend, or the consequences of a sin committed?

Has the thought of suicide crossed your mind?

How did you deal with that thought?

Do you feel like you have to earn the love of God like you would earn that of a friend, a teacher, or a perhaps parent?

In the light of today's Hot Button, explain the fallacy of that belief.

Do you know a friend who is struggling with self-worth and/or is suicidal?

A thousand teens attempt suicide every day. Learn to spot friends with such tendencies and intervene.

16   "That a Boy; That a Girl"

"His lord said unto him, Well done, good and faithful servant; thou hast been faithful over a few things, I will make thee ruler over many things: enter thou into the joy of thy lord."—Matthew 25:23.

He who trims himself to suit everyone will soon whittle himself away.[106]

Most people are other people. Their thoughts are someone else's opinions, their lives a mimicry [act of mimicking], their passions a quotation.[107]

Although we have responsibilities to others, we are primarily accountable to God. It is before Him that we stand, and to Him that one day we must give an account. We should not therefore rate human opinion too highly, becoming depressed when criticized and elated when flattered.[108]—John Stott

Too many students live their lives under the umbrella of another's approval. Their actions, attitudes, and aspirations are directly linked to how others think their lives should be lived. If they do as these people think, good feelings result, while failure to do so results in feeling miserable. This manipulative type approval leads to an emotional roller coaster of ups and downs, to an unhealthy view of one's own self-worth, to an eroding of confidence in one's own abilities, and often into various types of sinful activities.

How about you? Do you take cues regarding dress, speech, hairstyle, and activities from the expectations of others in an effort to please them?

If so, it is long past time for you to switch the source from which you seek approval. You see, the ultimate source of authoritative approval is God. It's what He thinks of you that counts most. All other sources of approval bow in subjection to Him. The foundational question, then, is not how others approve of your life, but how God does.

A young violinist, in ending his first concert, was applauded by a standing audience. Amidst the approval of the crowd, his eyes stayed fixed the entire time upon an elderly man in the balcony. The young violinist showed no emotion of joy until that man stood and applauded. You see, that elderly man was the young violinist's instructor, and he was only concerned with pleasing him.

Such was the attitude of the Apostle Paul with regard to Christ, for he testifies, "Obviously, I'm not trying to win the approval of people, but of God. If pleasing people were my goal, I would not be Christ's servant" (Galatians 1:10, NLT).

Live your life before an audience of ONE. If you please God with your life, it matters not if others accept you or not. All that matters in life, and then in death, is to hear our Lord say, "Well done, thou good and faithful servant" (Matthew 25:21), or, in modern translation, "That a boy," or "That a girl."

Another great danger in the church is imitation, the tendency of people to become like someone in the church they admire, or like some famous Christian[109]—not necessarily for approval, but for recognition or acclaim or well-intentioned accomplishment in ministry for Christ. In doing this, people destroy their own uniqueness.

The psalmist declares, "I will give thanks to You, for I am fearfully and wonderfully made; Wonderful are Your works, And my soul knows it very well" (Psalm 139:14, NASB). You are an original, incredible design of God. Fully grasp that, and rejoice in that! Don't succumb to the pressure to become a duplicate of someone else.

David could not wear King Saul's armor, nor can you wear another's.
Be who God made you to be.

ASK YOURSELF

Why does the approval or disapproval of another weigh so heavily upon you?

Whose disapproval would greatly hurt you? Why?

Outside of God being the ultimate authoritative source of approval, who else might be secondarily helpful?

Whom are you manipulating (innocently or purposefully) by forcing upon them your disapproval or approval?

Explain the Apostle Paul's statement cited in Galatians 1:10.

What is the great danger of imitation in the church? Why?

Watch J. J. Keller's video *Love Me for Me* on the Internet. Do you identify with the person described? If so, in what ways?

Who is speaking in the last two stanzas of the song, and how does that resonate with your heart?

17   Happily Dating without Hurtful Consequences

"Above all else, guard your heart, for it is the wellspring of life."—Proverbs 4:23, NIV.

Dating is not only a wonderful time of life, but also a context for enormous spiritual and personal growth. You learn so much about yourself, others, God, love, spirituality, and life through dating. Done well, it can be fulfilling, in and of itself. Done well, it can be one of the most fun and rewarding aspects of your life. Done well, it can lead to a good marriage.[110]—Henry Cloud

The key to happily dating without experiencing hurtful consequences is to allow God to govern the relationship from the get-go. It is essential to establish some well-defined boundaries prior to dating.

The person of dating. The decision to date a person must not be based simply upon appearance or emotional feelings, but also upon analysis of belief and conduct. Christians are to date only likeminded believers (2 Corinthians 6:14). The unequal yoke principle makes no allowance for missionary dating—the dating of unbelievers with intent to win them to faith. There are far safer arenas for soul winning than on a date.

Dating someone with whom you are "equally yoked" positions the relationship to be built upon biblical values and a firm foundation for marriage, should God so ordain. Date individuals who will be an asset rather than a deficit, a challenge rather than a conflict to your walk with God. Go out with individuals who have no hesitancy to pray with you prior to, during, or at the end of the date. It is expedient to check out thoroughly the person who invites you on a date or whom you invite for a date, primarily due to the fact that values must *mesh,* or else it will wind up a *mess.*

It is easy to get so emotionally bound to a person that you fail to think about how he or she lived prior to meeting you. It is easy to think of the person as so wonderful that there couldn't possibly be a blemish in the past. Thinking in this manner often ends in disaster and heartache.

Do your homework about a potential date by getting answers to these questions. How did this person treat former dates? What kind of reputation does he or she have in the locker room? Has your potential date ever used drugs or consumed alcohol? What is the person like in private, away from the public eye? How does he or she deal with an anger issue? Is the one you are considering dating a devout Christian, or simply a Christian in name only?

Often in relationships one cannot see "the forest for the trees" or "the big picture," bringing about the need for an unprejudiced caring godly person to voice an opinion from his or her vantage point. I hope this doesn't sound "uncool," but your parent(s) could fulfill this role. Additional insight may be gained by consulting with your student minister or pastor. "Without consultation, plans are frustrated, but with many counselors they succeed" (Proverbs 15:22, NASB).

The place of dating. Selection of the destination of the date must be settled (and approved) long before it is initiated. It is the "unplanned" date that often leads to the unplanned and later regrettable action. Plan the date, and stick to the plan. Avoid simply parking or being together alone at home, for it gives sexual passion the opportunity to ignite. It only takes a spark to get a fire going that often cannot be quenched until it does its destructive work. Gigantic trees which withstood rain, hail, and snow have been reduced to ashes by fire that began with a small spark.

The period of dating. Don't hesitate to break off a date the moment you feel uncomfortable or have second thoughts, for this is the Holy Spirit sounding the alarm to back down. In order for you to meet Mister or Miss Right, such relationships must end.

It is advisable to take date breaks periodically, especially if the relationship is moving far too fast, one or the other is becoming too serious, personal domination is exhibited, passionate petting is occurring, or sexual control is about to be lost. A physical and spiritual date break will clear the head, cool down the passion, conserve purity, and confirm whether or not the relationship should continue.

The procedure of dating. The date (including its plan) is initiated by the boy and accepted or rejected by the girl. The boy, neatly dressed and groomed and in a freshly washed and cleaned car, on the selected day, goes to the home of the girl and knocks on the door to pick her up. He does not toot the horn of the car. Customarily at this time, he will meet with the girl's parents, especially her father, to share plans for the evening, including the time of their return. The couple leaves the home for the planned activity and returns at the stated time. If an occurrence alters the time stated for the return, the boy notifies the girl's parents. The boy walks the girl to the door, making sure she is safe inside prior to departure.

The attire of dating. Dress plays a role in determining the degree to which one is confronted with sexual temptation. Revealing or skin-tight clothing heightens the risk of lust and sex. Dress modestly, not like a prostitute on the prowl. Young ladies, dress to bring attention to the face, not to the body.

The accountability of dating. To help insure moral purity in dating, align with a friend who will ask you the hard questions following the date. Knowing that you have to tell another person what transpired on a date builds in added resistance to the sex

81

temptation. Additionally, it is good to double-date for the sake of accountability.

How far is too far in dating? When I posed this question to a student gathering, one student responded, "When you hit a home run." To this student, all was fair game in dating, with the exception of having sex. How would you answer this question?

Obviously one has gone too far if he has engaged in sex with his date. That's a *no-brainer.* But it's possible to go too far long before reaching that point. You have gone too far if you are sexually aroused, if lust burns in your heart, if fondling occurs, or if conversation is initiated about having sex. The goal in Christian dating is to stay far removed from having these activities erupt by avoiding any act that spurs them to happen.

Additional hints to happy dating.

1. Avoid alcohol and drug consumption and places where such are consumed on dates.

2. Avoid drinking from opened containers that pass from another's hand due to the possibility that a date-rape drug has been introduced into it. Gamma-hydroxybutyrate (GHB) is a date-rape drug. It is invisible and odorless when dissolved in water. It's saltiness in low dosage is undetectable when introduced into a soft drink, beer, or liquor, but becomes more acute in higher dosages.[111]

3. Be stingy with displays of affection on dates. An occasional good night kiss, perhaps (save your kisses for your marriage partner), or holding hands is sufficient. Remember the law of diminishing returns is operable in dating—the more affection displayed now, the more that will be required later to satisfy.

4. I don't want to sound like a party-pooper, but the longer dating is postponed, the greater the chance is that virginity will be retained. A *Newsweek* survey revealed that 91% of girls who date at age 12 engage in sex prior to graduation, 56% of girls who date at

age 13 engage in sex prior to graduation, 53% of girls who date at the age of 14 engage in sex prior to graduation, 40% of girls who date at the age of 15 engage in sex prior to graduation, whereas only 20% of girls who wait to date until the age of 16 have sex prior to graduation.

5. Stay with the crowd and stick to the lights on dates.

6. Absolutely do not engage in Internet or blind dating. Check out thoroughly a potential date's dating track record.

7. At Camp Longridge, a ministry of the Frank Shivers Evangelistic Association, a movie entitled *The Pretender* has been shown to students. In this movie, a handsome young man pretends to be a Christian to get dates with Christian girls. Watch out for the *pretenders!* A person is known by the fruit displayed through his or her life.

8. Avoid feeling that you owe something to your date. This point is addressed toward the young ladies. Guys often will lead a girl to believe that they owe him some "action" because of the wonderful evening he provided. Girls, the next time a guy throws that number at you, give him a dollar and tell him to buy a hamburger! That's more than you owe him. The poor fellow really owes you respect and admiration for going out with him.

9. Never leave home without the cell phone in hand. If a guy gets too fresh, the girls can call dad; if a girl gets too fresh, the boys can call 9-1-1!

10. Finally, but certainly not least, pray regarding the dating encounter. Ask God for guidance about whom to date, for protection on the date, for moral restraint during the date, and for discernment as to when it is advantageous, spiritually and otherwise, to quit the date.

Dating can be a pleasant, enjoyable, and spiritually healthy experience, if these simple guidelines are heeded.

ASK YOURSELF

What is the "unequal yoke" principle of Scripture, and how does it apply to dating?

Why is missionary dating dangerous, and thus forbidden?

When is a date-break necessary?

What role does type of attire play in dating?

How far is too far in dating?

What places ought to be avoided on dates?

Who might be an accountability partner regarding dating conduct?

18   Choosing Whom to Marry

"Honest inside and out, a man of his word, who was totally devoted to God and hated evil with a passion."—Job 1:1, The Message.

"Who can find a virtuous and capable wife? She is more precious than rubies." —Proverbs 31: 10, NLT.

You know, the great miracle is not love at first sight. It is love after a long, long look.[112]—Adrian Rogers

I want to urge you to beware of being swept off your feet by what is called falling in love and assuming that that in itself is an adequate basis for marriage. There are some other considerations, such as intellectual compatibility. Is the person I find myself falling in love with a Christian, and a committed, mature and growing one? Is that person going to be a good father or mother to my children? Is that person going to be a good companion? Has that person my respect, as well as my physical desire? Now these are questions that the mind asks when the emotion of falling in love begins to well up inside me.[113]—John Stott

How old are you? If you are between twelve and sixteen years of age, you could be married in six years, or in only 2,190 days! Are you older? Then marriage is perhaps just around the corner. Crazy as it seems, now is the time to start preparing for that walk down the aisle. It will get here in a hurry.

Obviously, it is not God's will for everyone to marry. In 1 Corinthians 7, the Apostle Paul, in counseling the unmarried, makes it clear that they are not unspiritual because they are single. One version translates verse 1: "It is perfectly proper, honorable, morally befitting for a man to live in strict celibacy" (Wuest). It's okay to remain single (v. 8), provided the person has been given the "gift" (v. 7) of celibacy, a gift that Paul possessed.

Before the "hunt" for a life's mate begins, a guideline must be established regarding the selection criteria. You only get married once, and grave care, consideration, and caution must be manifested, so that marriage will be to the person of *your* dreams, not another person's dreams. James Dobson comments that the "threat of being an 'old maid' causes many girls to grab the first train down the marital track. And too often, it offers a one-way ticket to disaster."[114] Don't hurry; exhibit patience in waiting on God's timing to merge the right man or woman into your life.

How can you know Mr. Right or Miss Right? Mrs. Ruth Graham (deceased wife of the famed evangelist Billy Graham) told an audience, "God has not always answered my prayers. If He had, I would have married the wrong man—several times." Certainly if one as saintly as she had difficulty understanding God's will regarding whom to marry, you probably will also.

Seven Keys in Selecting a Husband or Wife

In selecting a life's mate, long prior to having to make a decision regarding marriage, walk in harmony with God and His Word. When Abraham's servant sought a wife for Isaac, God led him to Rebekah. Upon meeting her, the servant explained himself to Rebekah, saying, "I being in the way, the LORD led me" (Genesis 24:27). It is essential that you spend time "in the way"—in obedience and intimate communion with God—if you want to be led by God. Max Lucado states, "We learn God's will by spending time in His presence. The key to knowing God's heart is having a relationship with Him—a personal relationship."[115]

The second key that will clear the fog giving guidance in this matter is prayer. Wisdom and discernment are acquired through prayer. "But if any of you needs wisdom, you should ask God for it.

He is generous to everyone and will give you wisdom without criticizing you (James 1:5, NCV)." In other words, James says that the believer who wants to know God's will should go to Him saying, "God, I do want to fulfill your plan regarding my life's mate, but I need divine wisdom to know that plan." We cannot expect God to give the illumination we need if we don't ask Him for it.

Theologian J. I. Packer, in *Knowing God,* indicates that "wisdom" in Scripture always means knowledge of the course of action that will please God and secure life.[116] Solomon, too, insisted that believers rely wholly on insights from God.

"Trust the Lord with all your heart, and don't depend on your own understanding. Remember the LORD in all you do, and he will give you success. Don't depend on your own wisdom. Respect the Lord and refuse to do wrong."—Proverbs 3:5–7, NCV.

Third, along with asking for God's wisdom, you must set aside personal preference. It's not uncommon for a student to ask God for guidance, only to hear what he wants to hear instead of the real voice of God. John Wesley said, "I find that the chief purpose in determining the will of God is to get my will in an unprejudiced state about the issue at hand."[117] You must do exactly the same when seeking divine guidance regarding a marriage mate.

A fourth key to making the right decision about whom to marry is absorption of Holy Scripture. Mark this down. God will never lead anyone to do something, including marriage, that violates His Word. "The statutes of the LORD are right, rejoicing the heart: the commandment of the LORD is pure, enlightening the eyes" (Psalm 19:8). Holy Scripture transmits light (divine knowledge) to the soul. J. I. Packer states that "the fundamental mode whereby our rational Creator guides His rational creatures is by rational understanding and application of His written Word."[118]

A fifth key to marital guidance is others. Solomon states, "The way of a fool is right in his own eyes, but a wise man is he who listens to counsel" (Proverbs 12:15, NASB). Your parents don't want your marriage to be a hellish experience, but a happy one, so seek their wisdom and LISTEN! This key is imperative, since you cannot trust the heart. It has deceived you time and again and maybe in this case as well. Jeremiah describes the heart rightly. "The heart is deceitful above all things, and desperately wicked: who can know it?" (Jeremiah 17:9).

A sixth key is investigation. Politicians are known for vetting potential candidates for public office prior to nomination to make sure they are what they appear to be. It is not only sensible to vet a potential mate, but imperative. Far too many discover the person lying in bed next to them is a stranger after they say, "I do." Remember, some guys or girls will be or do whatever is necessary to win your hand in marriage, while all the time it is one big lie.

A seventh key is to be sure the selection of a life's mate is not based merely on infatuation, but on genuine love. Infatuation is based on fleeting feeling; love is based on emotion and the will. Infatuation is for a moment in time; love is forever. Infatuation is self-serving, seeking personal pleasure; love is selfless. Infatuation fades with separation; love grows. Infatuation is something one falls into; with love, one grows into it. The Bible gives the best definition and description of genuine love, and a deep study of it will reveal whether a person is merely infatuated with you or genuinely loves you (1 Corinthians 13:4–8).

Traits to Look for in a Life's Mate
1. Has a personal relationship with Christ
2. Has a devoted, surrendered heart to Christ
3. Has a servant's attitude
4. Is established in scripture
5. Embraces biblical convictions and exhibits godly conduct
6. Is a challenge to spiritual growth; adorned with godliness
7. Refrains from sex before marriage
8. Is willing to make sacrifices

9. Shares similar likes/dislikes (compatibility physically/spiritually/emotionally)

10. Is trustworthy, truthful and transparent

11. Is a gentleman/lady of the noblest kind (respect, courtesy, gentleness)

12. Is supportive of career choices

13. Is agreeable regarding having children or not

14. Provides total and loving acceptance

15. Shares similar heart vision for life and commitment to God

16. Displays "flexibility" with the stuff of life

17. Provides security (for girls' life's mates)

18. Stays far removed from the boundary line of sexual misconduct

19. Is one to whom you are not only physically attracted but spiritually (Holy Spirit) drawn

20. Is not given to alcohol, drugs or pornography

21. Has proven his or her ability to control anger

22. Is mature enough to handle the up and down issues of marriage

A Personal Pledge

For such a man/woman I pledge to wait and prepare for both spiritually and morally. With the help of God, I will be content with my singleness until He merges my life with His choice of a life's partner for me. I refuse to act rashly based upon my fleshy, sensual desires or yield to other pressures that may weigh upon my soul to push ahead of God. I refuse to date for merely sexual reasons or companionship, but do so only under His leadership that I might discover my life's partner. A godly mate is hard to find. I therefore am determined not to settle for second best, but to wait upon the Lord to bring this awesome person into my life.

Ask Yourself

What five top character traits do you deem most important in the selection of a life's mate?

Are "looks" the key essential in the selection of a marriage partner?

Why do you or do you not intend on getting married?

What role does God play in the selection of a life's mate?

Is it possible to push ahead of God and marry outside His will?

Once the decision is made to marry, is it acceptable to engage in sex prior to being married? Why or why not?

What are the seven keys to choosing the right person to wed?

19   Marriage and Divorce

"'Haven't you read the Scriptures?' Jesus replied. 'They record that from the beginning "God made them male and female,"' And he said, 'This explains why a man leaves his father and mother and is joined to his wife, and the two are united into one. Since they are no longer two but one, let no one split apart what God has joined together.'"—Matthew 19:4–6, NLT.

Divorce myths: 1) When love has gone out a marriage, it is better to get divorced. 2) It is better for the children for the unhappy couple to divorce than to raise their children in the atmosphere of an unhappy marriage. 3) Divorce is the lesser of two evils. 4) You owe it to yourself. 5) Everyone's entitled to one mistake. 6) God led me to this divorce.

Marriage is established and regulated by a God of truth. The problems of marriage cannot be resolved by myths.[119]—R. C. Sproul

Marriage is a divine institution established by God between a man and a woman, and it is designed to last a lifetime (Matthew 19:4–6). Jesus forthrightly stated that a husband and a wife were "one flesh" and that their marriage pictures His unending and abiding love for His bride, the church (Ephesians 5:24–31). Jesus is the "Bridegroom" of the church—the bride, the redeemed family of God—and this union will never be divorced.

Likewise, the husband and the wife are one flesh, united by God's ordaining authority, and their union must not be severed. "What therefore God hath joined together, let not man put asunder" (Matthew 19: 6). God said, "I hate divorce" (Malachi 2:16, NLT). The apostle Paul frankly said, "A wife must not separate from her husband" (1 Corinthians 7:10, NIV), and, "And a husband must not divorce his wife" (verse 11, NIV). It is noteworthy that Paul used the words "divorce" and "separate from" interchangeably.

No divorce from marriage was God's ordained design from "the beginning." The first couple, Adam and Eve, exemplifies God's will for marriage in that they remained united (Matthew 19:8). However, not long after the Fall of man, God's divine standard for marriage was violated (Genesis 2:24; 4:19). Jesus, in answering the questions of the Pharisees regarding the permissibility of divorce, emphatically stated that God's divine design for marriage from the beginning has not changed, that it was only due to the hardness of man's heart that Moses allowed it (Matthew 19:5–8; Deuteronomy 24:1–3). Careful reading reveals that Deuteronomy 24:1 doesn't sanction divorce, doesn't give a command to divorce, as some propagate.

Are there any circumstances in which one can change the "I do" said in a marriage ceremony to an "I don't" afterwards? Are there any legitimate grounds sanctioned by Scripture for divorce? Jesus grants an exception clause with regard to the no divorce standard in Matthew 19:9: "And I say unto you, Whosoever shall put away his wife, except it be for fornication, and shall marry another, committeth adultery: and whoso marrieth her which is put away doth commit adultery." The word "fornication" refers to all kinds of gross sexual immorality. Obviously this is equally applicable for the wife with regard to divorcing her husband.

The apostle Paul adds a second exception to the no divorce standard in 1 Corinthians 7:13–16 in stating that it is permissible for the husband or wife who becomes a believer in marriage to separate from their unbelieving partner, if the unbelieving spouse initiates it. However, Paul emphasizes in verse 16, if at all possible, that Christians should remain married to their unbelieving spouses in an effort to win them to Christ (verse 16).

Jesus' teaching on no divorce was so rigid and unbendable that the disciples said following the discourse in Matthew 19, 'It's best not to marry' (Matthew 19:10). Even the two "exceptions" for divorce are to be an absolutely last resort. Divorce is tragic and nearly always preventable. The person who divorces contrary to the guidelines of Scripture may not remarry, unless it is to his or her former spouse (Mark 10:11–12). An unbiblical divorce produces evil consequences (Matthew 19: 9).

The bottom line regarding marriage is that it is to last a lifetime with a single mate—not with multiple partners. When one's partner dies, then the person is free to marry again, as long as the marriage is "in the Lord" (1 Corinthians 7:39).

Grave consideration ought to be given in the choice of a life's mate; hasty and flippant weddings are to be avoided. God does not allow "trial runs." It is imperative that a man and a woman be equally yoked in believing faith in the Lord Jesus Christ in courtship and in marriage and that God sanction their union. In marriage, it is essential that the home be built upon biblical principles, worship and prayer; that the husband love the wife as Christ loves the Church (Ephesians 5:25); and that the subject of divorce never be broached. A husband or a wife is God's best gift to you, so marry in the Lord and enjoy the awesome life He has designed.

ASK YOURSELF

What was God's design for marriage from the beginning?

Has God changed His mind?

According to Malachi, God's attitude toward divorce is what?

If this is God's attitude, then why do you suppose there are about as many divorces among Christians as there are among non-Christians?

What are the only possible exceptions for divorce in Scripture?

What are some preventative measures against divorce that may be taken before marriage, and what measures are available while a couple is married?

What should be your attitude toward a divorced person?

20   Honoring Parents

"And the children shall rise up against their parents, and cause them to be put to death."—Matthew 10:21.

If you have committed your life to the Lordship of Christ, you have no other option. You must show honor [to your parents] at all times.[120]—Josh McDowell

We see Matthew 10:21 fulfilled in our day. Children rebel against God-ordained authority by refusing to submit to instructions and show respect for their parents. Parents are to be honored by their children, not cursed (Exodus 20:12).

You owe your parents life itself—their blood flows in your veins. They have loved you since conception and have gladly sacrificed greatly for you. You ought to love them unceasingly and show them the highest respect! Shakespeare said, "How sharper than a serpent's tooth it is to have a thankless child."[121] Disrespect and ingratitude are more venomous to parents than the bite of a rattlesnake. An ungrateful, defiant boy continually arrived home past curfew. One night his dad waited, holding a shotgun. As the boy entered the house, the dad tossed the gun to him and said, "Go upstairs, put the barrel to your mother's head, and pull the trigger."

Stunned, the boy replied, "Dad, what are you asking me to do?" When the father repeated the instructions, the son asked, "Why?" The father said that shooting his mother would be more merciful than the gradual, slow way he was killing her with rebellious behavior. Shakespeare is so right; your disrespect and disobedience to your parents are sharp fangs, mightier than those of a serpent and gradually killing them.

Deuteronomy 21:18–21 shows God's view of disobedience and disrespect toward parents: "If a man have a stubborn and rebellious son, which will not obey the voice of his father, or the voice of his mother, and that, when they have chastened him, will not hearken unto them: Then shall his father and his mother lay hold on him, and bring him out unto the elders of his city, and unto the gate of his place; And they shall say unto the elders of his city, This our son is stubborn and rebellious, he will not obey our voice; he is a glutton, and a drunkard. And all the men of his city shall stone him with stones, that he die: so shalt thou put evil away from among you; and all Israel shall hear, and fear."

This sentence of stoning a disobedient child was in the Old Testament, but it reveals God's expectation that children obey the fifth commandment: "Honour thy father and thy mother: that thy days may be long upon the land which the LORD thy God giveth thee" (Exodus 20:12). Notice also the promise God makes in the second part of this verse regarding children who obey their parents.

The greatest gifts one can give to parents are respect, obedience, and affection. "Children, obey your parents in all things: for this is well pleasing unto the Lord" (Colossians 3:20).

No parent bats 1.000; sometimes Mom and Dad will foul out, despite their best intentions regarding a matter. Regrettably, I know I did and had to ask my children's forgiveness. Cut your parents some slack when they blow it.

In addition to prompt and unquestioned obedience to your parents' commands, how else may you honor them? Honor them by always addressing them as Dad or Mom or the equivalent thereof—not by their first names. Honor them by responding to their questions with "Yes sir," or, "Yes ma'am," or, "No sir," or, "No ma'am." Never refer to your parents as "the old man" or "the old woman." As long as my parents lived, I always called them Dad and Mom and answered, "Yes sir; no sir", or, "Yes ma'am; no ma'am." Your parents hold the highest position on earth, greater than that of the president in the White House, for they are kings in *your* house. Honor their position by not besmirching their title or person.

Your parents may die suddenly, and with their death, opportunities for reconciliation, for expression of gratitude and love, for obedience, and for the blessings of their presence will forever be gone. Harriet Beecher Stowe (1811–1896), author of *Uncle Tom's Cabin,* said, "The bitterest tears shed over graves are for words left unsaid and deeds left undone."[122] Today, say what needs to be said and do what needs to be done to make things right with your mom and dad. Tomorrow, sadly, may be too late.

There is a song about a young man who led a wayward life, causing his parents much grief. Efforts by his parents to correct him prompted his angry departure, and he told them he would never return. Eventually this young man wound up in prison. Upon completing his sentence of many years, he decided to return home for a fresh start. Unsure of a welcome by his parents, he sent a letter to them seeking forgiveness and asking whether or not he could return home. Additionally, the letter stated he would be traveling by train by their house on a certain day. If he was welcomed home, they were to tie a yellow ribbon to a branch of the old oak tree in the front yard. The presence of the yellow ribbon would reveal whether he was wanted or not, whether he was to remain on the train or get off at the town's station. As the train neared the boy's home, due to fear of not seeing the yellow ribbon, he asked another to look toward his home for anything unusual. Upon doing so, the man saw yellow ribbons tied to every branch of the old oak tree.

You may be a runaway or one who has been away from home due to bitter disagreements with parents. It's past time to come home and make amends. There is no place like home. Your parents love you and welcome your return. In fact, I see yellow ribbons tied to every branch of the old oak tree in your front yard!

ASK YOURSELF

In what ways do you show respect for your parents? How did you show disrespect?

How strongly does God demand submission to and respect for parents?

Do you identify with the student who was breaking his mother's heart, slowly killing her with his disobedience?

Explain Shakespeare's statement that a 'thankless child is sharper than a serpent's tooth.'

If you are living in defiance to your parents, what is prompting it (friends, culture, or selfishness)?

If your parents were to die at midnight tonight, what would you wish you had said to them prior to their passing?

Why do you think that the child who honors his parents will live a long life?

Have you left home out of anger or resentment toward your parents? If so, what steps ought you to take in order to be reconciled with them?

Do you think they would hang a "yellow ribbon" of welcome out for you? Why or why not?

Keeping the Law - Nicodemus
The Rich young Ruler
The Apostle Paul
No One Can Keep the Law

21   The Ten Commandments

"And God spake all these words, saying..." Exodus 20: 1.

Not Moses, Not An Angel, Not A Prophet But God

If God would have wanted us to live in a permissive society, He would have given us Ten Suggestions and not Ten Commandments.[123] —Zig Ziglar

I have wondered at times what the Ten Commandments would have looked like if Moses had run them through the U.S. Congress.[124] —President Ronald Reagan

The moral code of Heaven for mankind is enveloped in the Ten Commandments (Exodus 20:2–17). The Ten Commandments provide **protection.** These laws or rules protect true theology and worship, the name of God and the Sabbath Day, family honor, life and marriage, property, truth, and virtue. They provide revelation.

The commandments are a **mirror** reflecting the sin in man's heart and his utter failure to live up to God's plan and purpose. Looking into this mirror, all have to say, "I am guilty. I must get right with God."

The Law is our **schoolmaster** to bring us to Jesus Christ (Galatians 3:21–26). Never was it intended to save man, but to show man his need to be saved. The commandments provide illumination, informing man about the character of God. He is a God who believes it is wrong to murder or steal or commit adultery or lie or treat another without respect. The commandments, therefore, are not just a list of prohibitions, but a theological "textbook" on what God is like.

Keeping The Ten Commandment The Rich young Ruler said I Have kept thae from my youth-

The commandments also provide **instruction,** teaching men what God expects of their lives—how they should treat others and Him. Each of these ten rules is for everyone personally. When God

99

says, "You shall not," He means *you*. No one can escape the consequences of noncompliance. Obey them and be rewarded; disobey them and be punished.

Here are the ten rules from the English Standard Version.

I. Rule One is **Love God More Than Anything**—"You shall have no other gods before me."

If we keep the first the other nine will be easy
This commandment is first in position because it is first in priority. Loving God with all the heart, mind, soul, and strength, and above all others, will make it easy to keep the other nine rules.

It is clear from this rule that the God of the Universe, Creator of Heaven and earth, and Sustainer of man demands and deserves a person's unrivaled love, worship, and obedience. But is He getting it? Are you guilty of placing love and affection in the created instead of in the Creator?

Have you ever wondered why no picture is status or Jesus of
II. Rule Two is **Worship God Rightly**—"You shall not make for yourself a carved image."

The first commandment tells us *whom* to worship; the second tells us *how* to worship. The first forbids false gods; the second forbids false worship.

The purpose of this rule is to keep the worship of God pure and true by worshipping God, not a representation of God. This command forbids the worship of anything God has made in nature, in the heavens or in the sea, and anything that is a "stand in" for Him. Don't worship God through a crucifix or a statue of Mary or a painting of Christ.

In order for worship to be pure and true, it must be focused totally upon God, not any representation of God. In raising our hands in worship, we are saying to God, "Our hands are empty. We worship only You; no carved images are in our hands."

The custom of folding the hands in prayer was derived from slaves who would bow before their masters to be shackled. Slaves, in doing this, were saying to their masters, "I am shackled to you, chained to you and only you in submission and service." In folding the hands in prayer before God, the believer is stating, "I always will belong to you and you alone."

Rule Three is **Don't Misuse God's Name**—"You shall not take the name of the Lord your God in vain."

It's impossible to separate a person from his or her name. In showing disrespect for one's name, disrespect for the person is manifested. In abusing God's name, a person is uttering disdain for God, whether intentional or not.

Use the tongue to magnify God's name, and thus His person—not to demean it. The lips are but the outlet of the heart, a mirror of the soul.

Rule Four is **Remember the Lord's Day**—"Remember the Sabbath day, to keep it holy."

The Chinese have a legend about a man who went into a village with a string of seven coins. In compassion, he gave six of these coins to a beggar and put the last coin in his pocket. The beggar happened to be a thief and a pickpocket who then stole the man's last coin.

Sadly, this is what many have done with Sunday. God has given man six days to work and play, yet he has taken God's day designed for worship and rest.

Rule Five is **Honor Your Parents**—"Honor your father and your mother."

God says, 'Honor your parents.' To "honor" means "to prize highly; to show respect, treat as precious or valuable." This commandment is discussed fully in Hot Button #20.

VI

Rule Six is **Do Not Murder**—"You shall not murder."

Murder is the taking of another's life in an unlawful way. This rule protects life from the moment of conception in the womb until death. Abortion is the murder of the age. Over forty-five million abortions occur annually globally. Doctors who perform abortions and others that encourage or have abortions will be held accountable by the Judge of the Universe.

A man died a drunkard's death. His friend said, "I killed him. I led him into dissipation. I was strong enough to take it, but he was not. I killed him." Perhaps he was right. Perhaps any person who leads another into a sin that leads to his death or to the death of another is guilty of murder.

The command does not prohibit killing in time of war, killing in self-defense, or the killing of animals for food.

VII

Your Body is The Temple Keep it clean

Rule Seven is **Keep Yourself Pure**—"You shall not commit adultery."

God forthrightly prohibits a married person from engaging in sexual acts with someone other than his or her marriage partner. Sadly, this aspect of God's moral code for mankind has all too often been violated, resulting in broken marriages, lives, and families.

This commandment is expanded by Jesus in Matthew 5:28 to include engaging in lustful thoughts.

VIII

Rule Eight is **You Shall Not Steal**—"You shall not steal."

There are five ways in which a person may break this commandment.

There is theft of property, the taking of something that belongs to another, regardless of its value or size. Stealing a piece of bubble gum is just as much theft as stealing a CD. Cheating on exams and in athletic contests are forms of stealing as well.

There is theft of reputation. In this case, it's not the hands that do the stealing, but the tongue. The tongue steals a person's reputation by uttering slanderous and injurious remarks.

There is the theft of purity. The sexual seduction of another violates this commandment in that one steals the person's treasure. Solomon states, "Stolen waters are sweet...but...her guests are in the depths of hell" (Proverbs 9:17–18). Are you guilty of this?

There is the theft of faith. Jeremiah said, "Is not my word like fire, declares the LORD, and like a hammer that breaks the rock in pieces? Therefore, behold, I am against the prophets, declares the LORD, who steal my words from one another" (Jeremiah 23:29, ESV). The person who takes the scissors of skepticism to clip the faith of another will be held accountable by God.

Many professors and teachers are guilty of this crime, and God will judge them harshly. Don't share spiritual doubts or questions with believers who are immature, for in doing so you may steal their faith before they have had time to be spiritually established.

There is the theft from God. How do we steal from God? Malachi answers that we do it by withholding from God our tithes and offerings (Malachi 3:8–10). Failure to give God His tithe is as much stealing as entering a neighbor's house and taking a television set.

There are no degrees of honesty. Either you are honest, or you are not honest. Which are you?

Rule Nine is **Don't Lie**—"You shall not bear false witness."

All the sin and trouble in the world began with lying. The Devil lied to Eve, and you know what happened. Lies put Jesus on the cross. In Ephesians 4:25, Paul tells us to, 'put away lying.'

A person lies when he utters an untruth. One may lie by insinuation or by exaggeration.

Someone said that a fish is not the only thing that grows after it is dead. Making your "fish" a little bigger, your achievement a little greater, to make yourself look a little better is a form of lying.

One lies by silence. An "I don't want to get involved" attitude can cost a man his reputation. If you know something that can help a man or lift a man, then it's your duty to tell it.

A person lies by disobedience. To promise God something and then fail to do it is a lie.

To sing songs to God that we do not mean is lying.

Failure to keep a pledge to a friend is a form of lying—things like a commitment to pray for someone or a promise not to divulge a confidence.

Do you remember the fairy tale of Pinocchio? Pinocchio's nose grew longer with each lie he told. What if that happened to your nose with each lie you told?

Rule Ten is You Shall Not Covet—"You shall not covet."

The previous four commandments prohibited acts which would harm another; this one prohibits all inordinate desire to have what belongs to another. It is coveting to say, "Oh, that I had his or her looks!"; "Oh, that I had his or her spouse!"; "Oh, that I had his gifts or her abilities!"; or, "Oh, that I had his wealth!"

This command simply means people should be content and happy with the manner in which God blesses them. Don't crave or lust for that which you cannot rightly have that belongs to another. God has promised to meet your every need. Don't doubt that He will.

The Ten Commandments remain the moral code of God for mankind despite their adulteration, neglect, ridicule, and the disobedience of many. The person that orders his or her life by these instructions will be divinely favored and blessed by God.

Those who do not do so will experience the judgment of God. In reality, when a person thinks he is breaking the commandments, they end up breaking him.

Ask Yourself

What are the four purposes for the Ten Commandments?

How are the commandments a mirror?

Without looking back, name the commandments and state what each one means. Once this is done, look back and check your answer.

The first five commandments deal with man's relationship to whom?

With what kind of relationships do the second five commandments deal?

What is the only commandment with promise?

What are some ways that a person may steal?

Why should lying be a big deal to you?

What commandment, if obeyed, will enable compliance to the other nine? Why?

22   How to Decide Questionable Things

"Whether therefore ye eat, or drink, or whatsoever ye do, do all to the glory of God."—1 Corinthians 10:31.

When you are faced with a questionable matter, approach several Christians individually and get their opinions. Their counsel is valuable in helping make the right decision.[125]—Curtis Hutson

Like me, you have no doubt on occasion asked, "Should I do this or not do this?" In such times, how are you to decide what to do? The honest answer to the following questions clearly should reveal the proper response.

Does it violate Scripture? "All scripture is given by inspiration of God, and is profitable for doctrine, for reproof, for correction, for instruction in righteousness" (2 Timothy 3:16). The Bible clearly identifies things that are wrong—and always will be wrong—from which we must abstain. When a matter is directly addressed in the Word of God, one's decision regarding it should be automatic, without further debate or discussion.

Can I do this in Jesus' name? "And whatsoever ye do in word or deed, do all in the name of the Lord Jesus, giving thanks to God and the Father by him" (Colossians 3:17). This is a principle that is most helpful in determining questionable things. Simply put, Paul is stating that whatever action being considered, whether by lip or life, must be done in Jesus' name (under His authority, with His blessing, as His representative), or be left undone.

Will it hurt others? "'We are allowed to do all things,' but not all things are good for us to do. 'We are allowed to do all things,' but not all things help others grow stronger" (1 Corinthians 10:23, NCV). The weaker brother principle (1 Corinthians 8:7–13)

states that one ought to refrain from any activity, even if it's okay to do it in and of itself, if it would cause a spiritually immature Christian to stumble. Love for others overrules personal liberty (Romans 15:2–3).

How does it appear to others? "Abstain from all appearance of evil" (1 Thessalonians 5:22). The appearance of wrong ought to be avoided as much as possible, for malicious gossip can be just as damaging to you as a wrongful act. Additionally, the appearance of wrong injuries the believer's testimony and damages his reputation. Apply this principle to places you go, people with whom you associate, and pleasures in which you engage.

Will it be a temptation? "Brothers and sisters, if someone in your group does something wrong, you who are spiritual should go to that person and gently help make him right again. But be careful, because you might be tempted to sin, too" (Galatians 6:1, NCV). Decisions about conduct should be based upon one's level of spiritual maturity, strength, and weakness. Sadly, many well-meaning believers, in trying to help others with a sinful habit they once had themselves, have fallen back into the same captivity. Avoid settings which pose a potential moral or spiritual threat.

Will it wound my conscience? "Cling to your faith in Christ, and keep your conscience clear. For some people have deliberately violated their consciences; as a result, their faith has been shipwrecked" (1 Timothy 1:19, NLT*).* The conscience is a wonderful "Checkpoint Charlie" regarding right and wrong, if it is saturated with the Word and mind of God and not seared [spiritually cauterized] by repetitive sinning (1 Timothy 4:2). Often the Holy Spirit will speak through the conscience about an activity or attitude, prodding our restraint. Oswald Chambers stated, "If I am in the habit of continually holding God's standard in front of me, my conscience will always direct me to God's perfect law and indicate what I should do. The question is, will I obey?"[126]

Paul disciplined himself to "have always a conscience void of offence toward God, and toward men" (Acts 24: 16), and so must every believer. In this connection, the Bible expositor Albert Barnes comments:

"Paul often appeals to his conscientiousness as the leading habit of life. Even before his conversion, he endeavored to act according to the dictates of conscience....To do that which is right, so that my conscience shall never reproach me. 'Void of offence.' That which is unoffensive or which does not cause one to stumble or fall. He means that he endeavored to keep his conscience so enlightened and pure in regard to duty, and that he acted according to its dictates in such a way, that his conduct should not be displeasing to God or injurious to man. To have such a conscience implies two things: (1) That it be enlightened or properly informed in regard to truth and duty; and (2) that that which is made known to be right should be honestly and faithfully performed...."[127]

Stay sensitive and obedient to God's stirrings to the conscience. "And the only thing that keeps our conscience sensitive to Him," writes Oswald Chambers, "is the habit of being open to God on the inside. When you begin to debate, stop immediately. Don't ask, 'Why can't I do this?' You are on the wrong track. There is no debating possible once your conscience speaks. Whatever it is— drop it, and see that you keep your inner vision clear."[128]

Will it stand at the judgment? "Every one of us shall give account of himself to God" (Romans 14:12). Decisions made will be judged at the Judgment Seat of Christ. Make sure your decisions at that hour will meet His approval.

Does it jettison or jeopardize my spiritual growth? "...but all things are not expedient" (1 Corinthians 6:12). Many things are acceptable, but are they spiritually beneficial to growth in Christ? Ask, "Will this activity be a help or hindrance in my pursuit of holiness, intimacy with God, and building up in the faith?"

ASK YOURSELF

Share an experience regarding a decision about a questionable activity. Did you make the right decision?

Which of the questions presented in the chapter serve to help especially in knowing what to do when Scripture *seems* to be silent about a matter?

Based upon the questions, what activities that you are presently engaged in should be stopped?

Have you caused or are you causing a weaker brother to stumble?

What is a "seared" conscience?

What role does the conscience play in decision making?

23   The Power of the Tongue

"But the tongue can no man tame; it is an unruly evil, full of deadly poison."—James 3:8.

Tongues are more terrible instruments than can be made with hammers and anvils, and the evil which they inflict cuts deeper and spreads wider.[129]—C. H. Spurgeon

In the classic movie *A Christmas Story,* during recess on a cold winter day, two boys surrounded by classmates argue whether a person's tongue will stick to the school's flagpole. One of the boys "triple-dog dares" the other to stick his tongue to the pole, and it gets stuck. As his classmates returned to class, there he remained with his tongue frozen to the flagpole in great pain. Of all the right uses of the tongue, this certainly was not one of them!

This humorous scene points out how the tongue misused brings trouble and pain. Solomon said, "Whoso keepeth his mouth and his tongue keepeth his soul from troubles" (Proverbs 21:23). Or, as The Message translation puts it, "Watch your words and hold your tongue; you'll save yourself a lot of grief." Whereas most students would not intentionally hurt another physically, they often do so mentally with the use of a vicious tongue.

The Bible speaks of the kinds of tongues that must be avoided because they will hurt God, others, and ourselves.

A Harsh Tongue. "A soft answer turns away wrath, but a harsh word stirs up anger" (Proverbs 15:1, ESV). I remember as a child saying to someone who had said something unkind to me, "Sticks and stones may break my bones, but words will never hurt me." I don't know why I ever said that, because their harsh words did hurt me. Harsh words are but an invisible sharp razor that cuts and pains the person on the receiving end deeply (Psalm 52:2).

A Lying Tongue. "The getting of treasures by a lying tongue is a vanity tossed to and fro of them that seek death" (Proverbs 21:6). In order to gain possessions, popularity, and/or friends, or to avoid punishment for acts committed, lies often are told. A lying tongue is condemned by God. Always speak the truth, despite the consequences.

A Belittling Tongue. "Do not use harmful words, but only helpful words, the kind that build up and provide what is needed, so that what you say will do good to those who hear you" (Ephesians 4:29, GNT). Never speak to someone in a way that makes them think they are a nobody. Words ought to lift another up, not pull them down. Who might you, without realizing it, be belittling with words?

A Betraying Tongue. "A gossip goes around telling secrets, but those who are trustworthy can keep a confidence" (Proverbs 11:13, NLT). Simply put, Solomon is saying, "Don't divulge what others have told in confidentiality, and never share such to hurt them openly." Determine to be a person who is trustworthy with secrets.

A Retaliating Tongue. "Don't repay evil for evil. Don't retaliate with insults when people insult you. Instead, pay them back with a blessing. That is what God has called you to do, and he will bless you for it" (1 Peter 3:9, NLT). "That goes for all of you, no exceptions. No retaliation. No sharp-tongued sarcasm. Instead, bless—that's your job, to bless. You'll be a blessing and also get a blessing" (The Message). When you are offended or injured by another's actions, refrain from striking back to get even. This is most difficult, for the flesh craves to even the score; but God says, "Don't do it; leave the matter to Me to handle."

God commands that we bless people who injure us. How? We bless others by praying for their salvation or spiritual progress, by expressing thankfulness for them, by doing something to help them, and by speaking well of them. God states that if we do that, not only will that person's life be enriched, but ours will be also.

"You can talk about me
As much as you please;
I'll talk about you
Down on my knees."

A Hasty Tongue. "Seest thou a man that is hasty in his words? there is more hope of a fool than of him" (Proverbs 29:20). "He that refraineth his lips is wise" (Proverbs 10:19). Be slow to speak, and learn when to be silent. When are the times that a person needs to refrain from speaking?

Hold the tongue when someone is angrily attacking you.

Hold the tongue when you are asked to do something that requires much thought and prayer. Don't answer hurriedly, for you could make a decision whether or not to do something that you would later regret.

Hold the tongue when being corrected by a parent or teacher instead of seeking to justify the wrong committed.

Hold the tongue when a parent gets on your case about something you count as petty. Remember, hasty speaking may lead to saying words you would later wish you had not said.

A Grumbling Tongue. "And when the people complained, it displeased the LORD: and the LORD heard it" (Numbers 11:1). To God's displeasure, the Israelites complained and grumbled in the wilderness about the manner in which He provided for them. There are few things worse than hearing a Christian grumble and complain, considering all God has done and is doing for them. The chorus to "The Grumbler's Song" describes them:

"Oh, they grumble on Monday, Tuesday, Wednesday; grumble on Thursday too.
"They grumble on Friday, Saturday, Sunday; grumble the whole week through."

In light of God's gracious provision, Solomon asks a most pressing question: "Then why should we, mere humans, complain" (Lamentations 3:39, NLT). Instead of complaining and whining, use the tongue to worship, adore, and praise God for all He has done and is doing for you. Nobody likes to be around a grumbler, not even God.

A Hollow Tongue. "A flattering mouth worketh ruin" (Proverbs 23:28). A flattering tongue sabotages trust and results in great hurt. Don't speak words of insincerity. Don't speak empty words. Be careful not to use the hollow tongue to praise people in order to gain approval or support. There is nothing wrong with sharing genuine, heartfelt compliments; just avoid stretching the truth, causing it to become a lie.

A Divisive Tongue. "He that soweth discord among brethren" (Proverbs 6:19). One of the seven things God hates is a person who uses the tongue to create dissension and discord. You sow discord by saying things that break bonds of friendship, promote cliques ("Us four and no more"), polarize one person from another (create a rift), and decay the trust that someone has in another.

A Discouraging Tongue. "And Judah said, The strength of the bearers of burdens is decayed, and there is much rubbish; so that we are not able to build the wall" (Nehemiah 4:10). Nehemiah was trying to rebuild the walls about Jerusalem and reestablish God's worship, which was opposed greatly. As if things were not difficult enough for Nehemiah, his right-hand man, Judah, spoke discouragingly, saying their effort was useless and they should quit. These words from Judah's mouth were like a sword to Nehemiah's heart. It has to be disheartening when a trusted friend, who should be inflating you to do what God has purposed, deflates you instead.

Don't use the tongue to discourage others from doing what God has placed in their hearts. If someone says God has called him to be a missionary, don't respond by saying, "You don't have what it takes to be a missionary"; instead, say, "I believe you will make a good one."

If someone says she is going to start a Bible Club at school, don't say, "Sure—that will be the day"; rather, tell her, "I was hoping someone would start a club, and I am glad you are that person."

If another says, "I am inviting Jesus into my heart to be my Lord and Savior," don't say, "I can't believe you are doing that." Encourage the person by saying, "I am so happy for you. Becoming a Christian is awesome."

Or, if someone states his decision to quit a certain sinful act (pornography, drugs, alcohol, gambling, sexual impurity, or something else), never respond, "You can't stop that. You can't change. You have tried before and failed, and you can't do it now either." Help him by telling him, "I know you tried to stop before, but I believe this time you will succeed with God's help."

Don't be a Judah. Rather, use the tongue to encourage people to do all God has placed in their hearts to accomplish. I wonder how many great things for God have gone undone because someone discouraged another person from attempting to do them.

Envision that in my hand is a pillow and that it's thousands of feathers are words. I am now cutting open the pillow and allowing the wind to blow the feathers everywhere. What are my chances of finding every single feather and replacing it in the pillow? Your words are like these feathers. Once they are spoken, they can never be taken back. Never use the tongue in the negative manners just discussed, and you will never be sorry for what you have said.

Muzzling the Tongue

So how can you "muzzle the tongue"? David states, "I will guard my ways, that I may not sin with my tongue; I will guard my mouth with a muzzle" (Psalm 39:1, ESV). How can you muzzle the mouth to say only things pleasing to God?

1. Be determined to abstain from the sins of the tongue.

2. Fill your mind with biblical, wholesome truth. What's in the well of the heart is what comes out its faucet (the tongue).

3. Lay the tongue on the altar of sacrifice. James tells us "no man can tame the tongue" (3:8, NIV). And he is right—but Jesus can. So rely upon His super-duper-natural strength to enable you to speak rightly (Philippians 4:13).

4. 'Don't give place to the devil' (Ephesians 4:27). That is, don't condone bad talk at any time about any person. Always say a loud NO to unhealthy talk.

5. Apply Greg Laurie's acronym T-H-I-N-K as a guide to healthy speech.[130]

T—Is it true? (Proverbs 12:17). If not, don't speak it.

H—Is it helpful, or hurtful? (Proverbs 12: 18).

I—Is it inspiring, uplifting, encouraging? (Proverbs 17:22).

N—Is it really necessary to say it at all? (Proverbs 13:2). Much of what is said about other people would be better left unsaid.

K—Is it kind, or demeaning? (Ephesians 4:32). Is it true, helpful, inspirational, necessary, and kind? If not, don't say it.

We all need to muzzle, bridle, control our tongues and use them more to tell others about Jesus and His awesome love. A good prayer for you to pray would be Psalm 141:3: "Set a watch, O LORD, before my mouth; keep the door of my lips."

Spurgeon states, "Slander, falsehood, insinuation, ridicule— these are poisoned arrows; how can we meet them? The Lord God promises us that, if we cannot silence them, we shall, at least, escape from being ruined by them. They condemn us for the moment, but we shall condemn them at last and forever. The mouth of them that speak lies shall be stopped, and their falsehoods shall be turned to the honor of those good men who suffered by them."[131]

Ask Yourself

Why is it that James states the tongue is difficult to tame?

Of the types of tongues described in this chapter, which ones have injured you? Which have you used to injure others?

Which of the tongues create the greatest damage and hurt?

In what ways are the words we speak like feathers from a pillow blown in various directions?

Explain the statement: Sometimes it is not *what* we say, but the *way* (tone) in which we say it.

What are hollow words, and why should they be avoided?

In what manner do the words one speaks relate to biblical morality?

What was the great fault of Nehemiah's friend Judah?

Are you a Judah, or has someone been a Judah to you?

How might a person control the tongue?

How can the wrong use of words create division in a youth group?

List some healthy/positive uses of the tongue.

In what manner ought the Christian to respond to the poisonous tongue?

How might you muzzle the tongue?

ENDNOTES

[1] C. H. Spurgeon. *Faith's Checkbook,* (New Kensington, Pennsylvania: Whitaker House, 2002), November 23 entry.

[2] John Ankerberg and John Weldon. *Handbook of Biblical Evidences*, (Eugene, Oregon: Harvest House Publishers, 1997), 63.

[3] John Stott. "Langham Partnership Daily Thought" (A Service of Langham Partnership International & John Stott Ministries), dailythought@langhampartnership.org, December 4, 2011.

[4] Glen Schultz. *Kingdom Education: God's Plan for Educating Future Generations*, (Nashville: LifeWay Press, 1998), 39.

[5] W. R. Moody, Ed. *Record of Christian Work—Volume XVII*, (New York: Fleming H. Revell Company, 1898), 535.

[6] "Pure Intimacy: The Effects of Prior Pornography Use on Marriage," www.pureintimacy.org/piArticles/A000000490.cfm, accessed November 21, 2011.

[7] "Christian Churches: Pornography Statistics Addiction & Industry," www.archomaha.org/pastoral/se/pdf/PornStats.pdf, accessed October 17, 2011.

[8] "Pornography Statistics," www.familysafemedia.com/pornography_statistics.html, accessed October 17, 2011.

[9] Ibid.

[10] 1986 Attorney General's Commission on Pornography.

[11] Cited by Dr. Phil Stringer, "The Pornography Plague," www.usiap.org/Viewpoints/Family/Morality/PornographyPlague.html, accessed November 18, 2011.

[12] J. L. McGaugh. "Preserving the Presence of the Past," *American Psychologist,* February 1983, 161.

[13] Cited in National Publications: Young Salvationist, www.salvationarmyusa.org. accessed November 18, 2011.

[14] Dr. James L. McDough cited in Kenneth Kantzer. "The Power of Porn," *Christianity Today,* 7 February 1989, 18.

[15] Cited in National Publications: Young Salvationist.

[16] Richard Land. "Walking in the Footprints of a Giant in the Faith," National Right to Life News. www.nrlc.org/news/2005/NRL12/Rogers.html, accessed November 23, 2011.

[17] John C. Willke (President, National Right to Life of Greater Cincinnati). *Abortion—Questions and Answers,* (Cincinnati, Ohio: Hayes Publishing Co., 1988).

[18] Laura Ingraham. *Power to the People,* (Washington: Regnery Publishing, Inc., 2007), 258.

[19] Ibid.

[20] Ibid.

[21] "What does the Bible say about abortion?" www.gotquestions.org/abortion-Bible.html, accessed October 15, 2011.

[22] The Bible and Abortion. Heritage House Literature, www.abortionfacts.com/literature/literature_9410cv.asp, accessed October 15, 2011.

[23] Ibid.

[24] Alexander Roberts and James Donaldson, Ed. *The Ante-Nicene Fathers,* (New York: Charles Scribner's Sons, 1905), 148.

[25] Degarmo and Key. "Who Will?" From the album, *The Pledge.*

[26] Lehman Strauss. "Homosexuality: The Christian Perspective." Bible.org, accessed November 7, 2011.

[27] Max Lucado. *Max on Life,* (Nashville: Thomas Nelson, 2010), 133.

[28] Dictionary.com, accessed November 27, 2011.

[29] Max Lucado. *Max on Life*, 132.

[30] Ibid.

ENDNOTES

[31] "SPEAK: Suicide Prevention Education Awareness for Kids," http://www.speakforthem.org/facts.html, accessed February 24, 2012.

[32] "Focus on the Family's Position Statement on Same-Sex Marriage and Civil Unions. June 15, 2010," www.citizenlink.com, accessed November 16, 2011.

[33] James Dobson. Focus on the Family Radio Broadcast (October 6, 2005).

[34] John MacArthur. "The Nucleus of Civilization," www.gty.org/Resources/Articles/A297, accessed November 18, 2011.

[35] John Edmiston. "Same-Sex Marriages, What Does the Bible Say?" Christiananswers.net, accessed November 7, 2011.

[36] Dietrich Bonhoeffer cited by Lust Quotes, christian-quotes.ochristian.com, accessed November 17, 2011.

[37] Thomas Fuller cited by Lust Quotes, christian-quotes.ochristian.com, accessed November 17, 2011.

[38] Frederick Buechner. *Godric*, (Harpers Collins Publishers: New York, 1980), 153.

[39] F. B. Meyer cited in www.preceptaustin.org/james, James 1:13–15 Commentary, accessed October 13, 2011.

[40] Shel Silverstein. *The Yipiyuk*, www.kalantarian.org/artak/Literature/Shel.htm, accessed March 9, 2011.

[41] John Piper. "ANTHEM: Strategies for Fighting Lust. November 5, 2001," www.desiringgod.org/resource.../anthem-strategies-for-fighting-lust, accessed March 8, 2011.

[42] Thinkexist.com, accessed November 26, 2011.

[43] "Feedbacks from Students about True Love Waits/Teen Testimonies," www.lifeway.com/ArticleView?storeId=10054...1...waits, accessed November 23, 2011.

[44] Ibid.

[45] E. Stanley Jones. *Abundant Living*, (Nashville: Abingdon-Cokesbury Press, 1942), 130.

[46] Cannon H. D. M. Spence and Joseph S. Exell, Ed. *The Pulpit Commentary (Genesis),* (London: C. Kegan Paul & Company, 1881), 449.

[47] John R. Rice. "At the Last." *Sword of the Lord,* (Murfreesboro, Tennessee: Sword of the Lord Publishers, February 28, 2003).

[48] Cited in *The Sword of the Lord,* Shelton Smith, Ed. (Murfreesboro, Tennessee: Sword of the Lord Publishers, November 25, 2011), 9.

[49] David L. Brown. "Seven Good Reasons Christians Should Not Drink." (1989 and February, 2002), www.logosresourcepages.org/Believers/drinking.htm, accessed November 20, 2011.

[50] Ibid.

[51] Ibid.

[52] *The Pulpit Commentary.*

[53] cited by Wolldave Rambo. "The Big Lie about Moderate Drinking," *Pageant Magazine,* (Orlando: Daniel Publishers, 1973, reprint), 3.

[54] cited by Glenn D. Everett. "Brain Damage Starts With the First Drink," Report of the Research by Dr. Melvin H. Kinsely, Charleston, South Carolina.

[55] cited by Chuck Phelps in *Voice of the Evangelists*. "Should Christians Drink in Moderation?" www.voiceoftheevangelists.com, accessed June 21, 2011.

[56] Paul Tan. *Encyclopedia of 7700 Illustrations,* (Rockville, Maryland: Assurance Publishers, 1979), 121.

[57] John Greenleaf Whittier Quotes, www.goodreads.com/author/quotes/267703.John_Greenleaf_Whittier, accessed October 16, 2011.

[58] Paul Tan. *Encyclopedia of 7700 Illustrations,* 125.

[59] Josh McDowell and Bob Hostetler. *Josh McDowell's Handbook on Counseling Youth,* (Nashville: Thomas Nelson, 1996), 407.

[60] VH1 Video Interview, March 28, 2000.

---

[61] Vernon J. Geberth. *Forensic Science University Package: Practical Homicide Investigation, Fourth Edition,* (Boca Raton, Boston, London, New York, Washington, D.C.: CRC Press, 2006), 438.

[62] Sex, and Drugs or Alcohol, www.josh.org, accessed November 21, 2011.

[63] Edward T. Welch. *Addictions: A Banquet in the Grave,* (Phillipsburg, NJ: P & R Publishing, 2001), 11–12.

[64] R. C. H. Lenski. *The Interpretation of St. Paul's Epistles to the Colossians, to the Thessalonians, to Timothy, to Titus and to Philemon,* (Columbus, OH: The Wartburg Press, 1956), 363.

[65] Quotes on Gambling Addiction, www.encognitive.com/node/24, accessed November 21, 2011.

[66] Ibid.

[67] John MacArthur. "Gambling: The Seductive Fantasy, Part I, (GC 90-164)," www.biblebb.com/files/MAC/90-164.htm, accessed March 5, 2011. [This sermon depicts the biblical reasons why gambling is a sin]

[68] Harvard Medical School Division on Addictions cited in The Oklahoma Association of Gambling Awareness, www.oagaa.org/html/statistics.htm, accessed March 5, 2011.

[69] R. Stinchfield. "Problem and pathological gambling among college students," www.edst.purdue.edu/faculty.../GamblingChapterStinchHanOls.pdf, 64.

[70] "Teen Gambling." Teenhelp.com, www.teenhelp.com, accessed March 5, 2011.

[71] R. Stinchfield. "Problem and pathological gambling among college students," 64.

[72] National Council on Problem Gambling. "Ten Questions about Gambling Behavior," www.robertperkinson.com/teen_gambling.htm, accessed March 5, 2011.

[73] Wikipedia Encyclopedia. "Problem Gambling," en.wikipedia.org/wiki/Problem_gambling, accessed March 8, 2011.

[74] Smoking Quotes and Sayings, www.coolnsmart.com/smoking_quotes, accessed November 22, 2011.

[75] Freedom from Smoking online, www.ffsonline.org, accessed November 22, 2011.

[76] Kathleen Meister. "Helping Smokers to Quit: A Role for Smokeless Tobacco?, October 10, 2006," www.acsh.org, accessed November 22, 2011.

[77] www.nlm.nih.gov/medlineplus/smoking.html, accessed March 4, 2011.

[78] American Cancer Society. *Cancer Facts and Figures, Report to the Public,* (New York, New York, 1983), 15.

[79] "Teen Smoking Facts," www.smoking-facts.net/Teen-Smoking-Facts.html, accessed March 4, 2011.

[80] "Types of Tobacco," www.oralcancerfoundation.org/tobacco/types_of_tobacco.htm, accessed March 5, 2011.

[81] Terry Martin. "Smoking Facts for Parents and Teens." (About.com Guide. Updated June 28, 2010), accessed March 4, 2011.

[82] Cited by the University of Bristol in England in "Smoking Shortens Your Lifespan," www.health.com, accessed March 5, 2011.

[83] Ibid.

[84] Paul Tan. *Encyclopedia of 7700 Illustrations,* 246.

[85] "The Case against Smokeless Tobacco: Five Facts for the Health Professional to Consider." *Journal American Dental Association, 1980,* www.ncbi.nlm.nih.gov/pubmed/6932432, accessed November 26, 2011.

[86] "Smokeless Tobacco," kidshealth.org, accessed November 23, 2011.

[87] "Smokeless Tobacco," teens.webmd.com/features/smokeless-tobacco, accessed March 5, 2011.

[88] Cited by the National Cancer Institute in "Types of Tobacco."

ENDNOTES

[89] Nancy Schimelpfening. *Teen Smoking Facts*. (About.com Guide. Updated May 4, 2009), accessed March 5, 2011.

[90] Ibid.

[91] "Rock Music, Report of Light Youth Ministries" (Tulsa, Oklahoma), 5.

[92] cited by David Bowie, *Rolling Stone,* February 12, 1976.

[93] Alan Bloom. *The Closing of the American Mind,* (New York: Simon & Schuster, 1st Touchstone edition, 1988), 68.

[94] "Rock Music, Report of Light Youth Ministries," 6.

[95] "Quotes about Suicide Prevention," www.yourlifeyourvoice.org/DiscoverIt/Pages/Quotes.aspx, accessed November 23, 2011.

[96] Ibid.

[97] Diane Eble. "The Warning Signs of the Suicidal," *Campus Life,* October, 1986, 18.

[98] *Suicide Awareness, Prevention, Intervention and Counseling—An Action Plan,* (Rochester, Minnesota: The National Suicide Help Center, 1987), 20.

[99] cited by Charles A. Twardy. *Suicide: The Preventable Death,* (Columbia, South Carolina: The State, March 21, 1989), Section B, 4.

[100] Timothy Faulk. personal correspondence, December 15, 2012.

[101] Ibid. (bracket content added).

[102] Ibid.

[103] Gregg Lewis. "Good News about Me." *Campus Life,* October, 1986, 30.

[104] Earliest known version cited in *Mother Goose's Melody* published in 1803, which has the modern version with a different last line: "Could not set Humpty Dumpty up again," en.wikipedia.org/wiki/Humpty_Dumpty, accessed May 30, 2011.

[105] "PastForward: The Truth about Suicide," healpastlives.com/pastlf/quote/qusuicid.htm, accessed November 23, 2011.

[106] Being Yourself Quotes and Sayings, coolnsmart.com, accessed November 23, 2011.

[107] Ibid.

[108] John Stott. "Langham Partnership Daily Thought," October 23, 2011.

[109] Warren W. Wiersbe. *The Bible Exposition Commentary, Vol. 2,* (Wheaton, Illinois: Victor Books, 1989), 439.

[110] Henry Cloud. *How to Get a Date Worth Keeping,* (Grand Rapids: Zondervan, 2005), 30. [The author does not agree with all the advice stated in this work]

[111] "U.S. Drug Enforcement Administration," en.wikipedia.org/wiki/Date_rape_drug, accessed May 25, 2011.

[112] Adrian Rogers. "Seven Secrets of Lasting Love," LWF.org. Accessed November 23, 2011.

[113] John Stott. "Langham Partnership Daily Thought," December 11, 2011.

[114] James Dobson. *What Wives Wish Their Husbands Knew About Women,* (Wheaton: Tyndale House Publishers, Inc., 1997), 96.

[115] Max Lucado and T. A. Gibbs. *Grace for the Moment: Inspirational Thoughts for Each Day of the Year,* (Nashville, Tennessee: J. Countryman, 2000), 218.

[116] J. I. Packer. *Knowing God,* (Madison, Wisconsin: Intervarsity Press, 1977), 211.

[117] In Dan Hayes, "Motivating Reasons to Pray," www.startingwithgod.com, accessed January 8, 2008.

[118] J. I. Packer. *Knowing God,* 214.

[119] R. C. Sproul. *The Intimate Marriage,* (Phillipsburg, New Jersey: P & R Publishing, 2004), 103–110. (Sproul gives reasoning for calling these myths in this work.)

[120] Josh McDowell and Bill Jones. *The Teenager Q & A Answer Book,* (Nashville: Thomas Nelson, 1990)

ENDNOTES

[121] William Shakespeare. *King Lear. (Act I, Scene IV, 13),* nfs.sparknotes.com, accessed May 25, 2011.

[122] Chuck Gallozzi. "Saddest Words," www.personal-development.com/chuck/saddest.htm, accessed October 16, 2011.

[123] ThinkExist.com, accessed November 23, 2011.

[124] Ibid.

[125] Curtis Hutson. *Deciding Questionable Things for the Christian,* (Murfreesboro, Tennessee: Sword of the Lord Publishers, 1983), 24.

[126] Oswald Chambers. *My Utmost for His Highest,* May 13.

[127] Albert Barnes. *Barnes on the New Testament, Vol. 3,* 333.

[128] Oswald Chambers. *My Utmost for His Highest,* May 13.

[129] C. H. Spurgeon. *Faith's Checkbook,* November 16 entry.

[130] Greg Laurie. "T.H.I.N.K," blog.greglaurie.com/?p=2990, January 28, 2010.

[131] C. H. Spurgeon. *Faith's Checkbook,* November 16 entry.

CPSIA information can be obtained at www.ICGtesting.com
Printed in the USA
LVOW090840110712

289459LV00003B/1/P